THE MANY FACES OF ALCOHOL

THE MANY FACES OF ALCOHOL

Ted Jackson

iUniverse, Inc.
New York Lincoln Shanghai

THE MANY FACES OF ALCOHOL

iUniverse, Inc.

For information address:
iUniverse, Inc.
2021 Pine Lake Road, Suite 100
Lincoln, NE 68512
www.iuniverse.com

ISBN: 0-595-33177-7 (pbk)
ISBN: 0-595-78013-X (cloth)

Printed in the United States of America

Contents

INTRODUCTION

I'm Ted and I'm an alcoholic. As I begin this document I have been sober for only two weeks. My original intent was to write up something to help me remain sober—to serve as a reminder when the cravings become too much to handle and also to remind me of how alcohol has gradually taken over my life. I've spent many years attempting to control alcohol while it already had me in its grip and was squeezing harder and harder. I envy people who are able to take a couple of drinks and possibly even get somewhat intoxicated on occasion. At one time I was like that—actually for about 10 years or so. During that time I would often only drink on weekends with an occasional beer or maybe a mixed drink during the week. Gradually I became a problem drinker and I really don't know where the fine line lies between problem drinkers and alcoholics. There are many signs of alcoholism but I consider the following as the most significant:;

- A tendency to drink alone
- A tendency to drink when the party is over
- having to have a drink in the morning after drinking heavily the previous night
- "stashing" bottles
- drinking hard liquor straight from the bottle

My wife's late Uncle was an alcoholic but he hadn't had a drink in 30 years. He gave me some good and simple advice. He said, "If you have any doubts about being an alcoholic just go to the liquor store and get a couple of fifths.—then just see what happens. "I actually tried this but finished one of the fifths the first day. I was so disgusted with my myself that I threw both bottles in the garbage—one empty and one full. You can probably guess what I did the next morning as soon as my wife left for work. I started going through the garbage looking for the bottle that was full. Once I had the bottle you certainly know what happened—I drank it. First of all I needed a drink to quell the hangover—then needed a drink because of something else. This rationalizing went on all morning and then I gave up and just drank the rest of the bottle. I even tried to rationalize this with some pretty flimsy excuses. After I finished my fifth I actually went to the to the liquor store and got another bottle to quell the hangover the next morning. I was so intoxicated that I was actually cross-eyed. Obviously I had no business being on the road at all. I was driving when I could barely walk. When I get to this cross-eyed state I know that I've had too much. to drink. I have to drive with one eye closed or I see two of everything. I even see two lines down the middle of the road. and have to close one eye in order to determine which is the true line. Anyway I bought 3 fifths in two days. I'm. amazed that the clerk at the liquor store would let me buy anything as I could hardly walk. How could I even doubt that I was an alcoholic? When I got that third bottle I, of course vowed that this would be my last bottle—a vow that I had broken countless times. Practically every time I bought a bottle it was to be my last one. I had a counselor who had a good idea.—if someone offers you a beer just think to yourself, "I don't want one beer, I want 20." The same holds true for cocktails, You don't want one—you want the whole bottle. Another sign of alcoholism occurs when you start "stashing" bottles. Once I even had one in the toilet tank. I suppose that there are still bottles stashed around the house somewhere. What was frustrating was when I couldn't remember where I had stashed a bottle. This happened to me one time. I finally gave up my search and just went to the liquor store. I was horrified to find out that the store was closed because of some election that was going on. I went home and more or less tore the house apart as well as the garage. Finally I gave up and went and got a 12 pack of beer. I really never liked beer that much because I couldn't drink enough to get me high. Somebody once told me that you have to be sober for 6 months before you would know what sobriety is like. I did indeed do these months but it was more of just a matter of proving to myself and my wife that I could do it. After 6 months I still craved alcohol and began right were I'd left off or even worse. Just will power didn't do the job for me. Finally I read the 12 steps of AA and began trying to put them into action. I will talk about the 12 steps a little later. Right now I want to tell you the story of my life as an example of what alcohol has can do to a person. Some of the stories I'm going to tell are quite funny but pathetic at the same time. I'm 60 years old now but am trying to make a new start (without alcohol). With the help of my higher power, God, I hope to be successful.

There are, of course, literally hundreds of books about alcoholism and I don't know that this book provides anything brand new. All alcoholics are different except for the common problem. Therefore there are many ways to view alcoholism and I hope only to add a few of my of own thoughts and describe some of my experiences. If

I can help just one person with this problem then the effort is worthwhile.

1

MY STORY

1 grew up in a devout Mormon family in Salt Lake City, Utah—the home of the Mormons. Such a family is somewhat insulated from the outside world and it's sins. I never questioned but always attended church meetings simply because my parents insisted that I do so.

Alcohol was, of course, disallowed. I also never questioned this but was somewhat disturbed by the fact that alcohol and smoking were practiced during the early days of the church. Did God change his mind or what.? However, who am I to question God? There is s passage in the bible that goes something like this "My thoughts are not your thoughts and my actions are not your actions". Still I was bothered by the fact that not drinking or smoking seemed to be the main measures of a good member. What about the two greatest commandments—love God and love your fellow man?

When I was about 10 a friend and I stole a can of beer from his dad's refrigerator. I tasted it and thought it was the worst thing I'd ever tasted. I couldn't imagine people actually drinking the stuff and liking it. Believe me I wish I still had that feeling. At any rate I was a good boy for about 23 years. I even went on a Mormon mission to Germany for two and a half years. I was about 21 and on my mission when a rather bizarre thing happened. As my mission companion and I were walking through a carnival we saw an interesting game. The idea was to toss a ping-pong ball into the feathered end of a badminton birdie. If you were able to do this you got whatever prize was under the birdie. I was successful on my first try and you can probably guess what my prize was—a bottle of wine. We couldn't decide what to do with it. Obviously we should have simply thrown it away but I think neither of us wanted to do that. We finally decided to take it back to our room and use it as a centerpiece for our table. I'm sure our landlady saw it while cleaning and she must have wondered what we were doing. At any rate we got a surprise visit from our zone leader and his companion. They immediately noticed the bottle of wine and I thought about saying that it was just a special grape juice. Later I learned that my companion was having the same thoughts, particularly because the label was incomprehensible. Finally we told the truth—the entire story. They immediately ask why we hadn't at least dumped the wine down the toilet…Our only defense was that we wanted the bottle as a centerpiece for our table. They more or less ordered us to get rid of the bottle. We did so but certainly not in the way that they had in mind.

There was one more episode concerning alcohol while I was on my mission. We were invited into a man's house and he offered us something to drink. We told him that we didn't drink alcohol and he said that he would give us some grape juice. Soon he appeared with our drinks. I tasted mine and immediately drank it. My companion took a sip and then remarked about the strange taste. By that time I was already on my second glass. I knew what we were drinking but said nothing. My companion had obviously never tasted alcohol but he finished his glass. He then asked the man if there was any alcohol in the drink. The man replied "yes but not enough to worry about". My companion immediately headed for the door without a word. I apologized to the man and explained the situation. He seemed to be a open-minded msn who would have certainly listened to what we had to say. I argued this point with my companion but he was obstinate and refused to go back. I felt that we had missed a golden opportunity. For the rest of my mission I was a "good" boy. However I didn't have what Mormons call a "testimony". I don't how many times I heard this "I know beyond the shadow of a doubt that the Mormon church is the only true church on the face of the earth". I've met too many wonderful people who are not Mormon and I can't imagine God ignoring their good works simply because they belong to the wrong church. At any rate whenever I "bore my testimony" I would say that I truly believed that the Mormon church was true but would never say that all other churches were false. I still believe that good people in any church will be rewarded for their good works. I envy those who say that they know beyond the shadow of doubt that the Mormon church is the only true church on the earth. What a good way to simplify your life. One thing I will never be able to understand is the questioning of the church by its members. Since the Morman church believes in current revelation to its prophet who is the argument really with. It's with God of course and I personally don't want to argue with HIM. It seems to me that some people view the church as a type of political platform aimed at pleasing the largest amount of people. Shouldn't God have a say in the matter. As far as I'm concerned if you don't agree with the church then leave it before starting protest marches, etc.

In my mission the emphasis was on baptisms and nothing else, I knew of one case of where a girl was baptized because she believed that one of the missionaries was going to send for her after his mission. However I don't know if she was just assuming this or if a missionary had somehow led her on. I would hate to think that the missionary actually promised this. At any rate I believe that this girl was baptized for the wrong reason. She was converted to the missionary rather than to the church. It is my opinion that missionaries shouldn't convert people. They should just give them information and support and let them covert themselves. I did baptize a young couple who came to believe that the church was true. My main concern was to get tradition-bound people to start thinking for themselves. The German population was roughly half Catholic and half Lutheran. I don't know how many times we heard something like this; "My grandfather was Catholic, my father was Catholic and I'm Catholic. Why should I change?"

Now let's move on to the next two years—the years between my mission and my tour of duty in the army. A few months after my return from the mission I was with two other returned missionaries. We were going to a softball practice when we stopped at a drive-in and got some cokes in paper cups. The other guys drank about half of the cokes, produced a bottle of bourbon and poured a good shot into in their cups. They also poured some into my cup and I didn't complain. After that whenever we went to softball practices or even games we went through the same procedure. We told ourselves that were just loosening up for the game, etc. We actually felt that alcohol was enhancing our performance. I also began drinking before golf rounds. At one time I played in a church golf tournament and was rather plowed when we started. Still I eagled the first hole and birdied the next two. By that time the effect of the alcohol was gone and I was beginning the inevitable hangover. I wish that I could say that the rest of the round was terrible but I was still hitting the ball well and won the tournament by several strokes. I amused myself by watching high ranking church officials building little tees in the sand traps.

When I was in a bowling league I even drank before bowling. Beer was served in the alley but that wasn't enough for me. I would always have a bottle in my car from which I would take a couple of healthy swigs before entering the alley. Then I would consume about 6 beers while bowling. I probably wandered a little during my approach to the foul line but still scored well. Obviously and foolishly I was beginning to feel that alcohol did allow me to perform better at athletic activities. I wonder now how much better I could have performed had I not drank. I even drank before basketball games but my shots were still going in. I did notice that I got tired a lot quicker than if I had been sober before the game. Gradually I began to feel that alcohol was not really augmenting my athletic prowess but was actually hurting it. The final straw came just a few years ago when I played in a softball game. I had my usual shots of vodka before the game. Notice that I was now drinking vodka straight out of the bottle. My hitting never suffered from alcohol but an incident in the outfield discouraged me from drinking anything but beer before or during an athletic event. I was playing outfield when a ball was hit to me. It was just a routine fly ball and I only had to move a few steps to catch it. I stumbled and the ball bounced off my head. There was absolutely nothing to stumble over. but I explained to my teammates that I had stepped into a sprinkler hole. I don't know if anyone believed me as I had always been a good outfielder.

Alcohol is no respecter of intelligence, etc. I had always been a good student. In junior high I got my name on a plaque for being the best scholar-athlete in the school. In high school I had a 3.96 GPA. I would have been considered a nerd except for the fact that I was also a good athlete. I also had did very well in my first year of college (before I went on the LDS mission).

I suppose the real reason I began drinking was the fact that I found that it did away with my inhibitions and made me more gregarious. I have always been a shy person and alcohol suppressed my shyness so that I had the confidence to ask a girl to dance and to try and arrange a date or at least get the her phone number. This is a good example of how alcohol can give one a false sense of confidence.

Now let's get back to the two years between my mission and the time I was drafted. I have already addressed the subject of how I really began drinking not long after I arrived home from my mission. The first time I got really drunk I didn't how I could make it into the house without someone waking up and I certainly didn't want to confront my parents in the shape I was in. Somehow I managed to get in the house although I had some trouble getting my key into the lock. Once in the house and being as quiet as I could, I staggered down to my bedroom. I came very close to falling down the stairs which would have been a real disaster.

At that time I confined my drinking almost exclusively to weekends. My friends and I would warm up with a few drinks and would then go to a dancing bar or to any dance that we knew of. We would dance with girls and at least get their phone numbers. Then we would call them and arrange a date. We really had only had object in mind and I'm sure you know what that was.

After about a year and one half into the two years I realized that I was going to be drafted as soon as I turned 24. After your 24th birthday you were no longer eligible for school deferments. I even tried get into ROTC which would have allowed me to finish college. before serving in the army. My hope was that the Vietnam war would be over before I had to put in my time. I finished with very high scores on their tests but still wasn't selected. There were just too many of us trying for a few slots. I suspect also that I blew the interview by not giving the high-ranking officers the answers or the respect that they were looking for.

As I faced the draft my whole attitude changed. Being the pessimist that I am, I figured that my fate was going to Vietnam and being killed. I decided to try to make up for lost time. I was already something of a drinker and this just exacerbated the problem. I certainly didn't want to die a virgin so my friends and I continued going to dancing bars and getting phone numbers. We would take the girls out on weekdays unless they were something special and it's hard to find something special in a bar. University dances were much better for finding something worthwhile, I still only drank on weekends for the most part but this soon changed. I enrolled for spring quarter at the University of Utah because I would have been immediately drafted had I not done so, However I very seldom went to class. Of course I failed all of my classes except for one which had a multiple choice final. I have always been either good or lucky on multiple choice tests. and I ended up with a score that allowed me to pass the class with a "D".

I had a job in which I was free to come and go as I pleased. What I started doing was just working half a day to get enough money to get by on. Afternoons would always find me on the golf course where I supplemented my income by playing "skins". I wish I had the golf swing that I had then. With so much golf playing I became quite good. Incidentally I didn't drink while playing golf except when a concession truck would come around and then I would get a cold beer. I would do my serious drinking at night and would awake with a hangover which would dissipate as the morning went on. By noon I was ready to play some more golf. Despite the drinking I was doing I don't think I was an alcoholic at the time. This will become evident as I continue to tell my story. I could either not drink or drink. I chose the latter as it was more fun but sometimes went for several days at a time without liquor or beer. I worried sometimes about becoming an alcoholic but then said to myself,: "What the hell—I'm going to get killed in Vietnam anyway!"

When I reached my 24th birthday on June 19, 1968 1 would get the mail every morning and look for my Uncle Sam letter. As time went on I began to think that I had managed to slip through a crack or something, Then in August my draft notice did come. The first thing I had to do was to take a pre-induction physical examination. I was actually hoping that the doctors would find something that would classify me as 4F, a class which meant "unfit for duty". It was a surprise when I met the younger brother of one of my best friends there. One doctor asked why his calves were shaved. The answer came back" "Have you ever heard of football—they tape us", This boy, despite being the University quarterback somehow got out on a 4F. He went on to quarterback the University for several years and then played several seasons for the Denver Broncos.

The army was a really a wake-up call. At the barracks we were herded off the truck like cattle and everyone seemed to be yelling at us to hurry, etc. Needless to say we weren't allowed to drink during basic training. We couldn't even have a soda pop or a candy bar. On one occasion, after a 10 mile forced run\walk we were each given one beer with our evening chow. There was one exception besides the one that I just mentioned. Everyone who fired expert on the rifle range (there were only two from my company) got a special treat. We joined up with the rifle experts from some other companies and were taken to the PX where we had two hours to eat and drink anything we wanted. I started off with two packages of Twinkies and then a candy bar. Then I started on the beer. The other guy from my company kept count and told me later that I had drank 26 beers but that he had to quit after 19. Our march back to the barracks must have been a sight to behold. We were staggering all over the place and the corporal who was watching over us was just about as drunk as we were. He let one of us do the cadence songs and this guy was certainly creative. He used every "bad" word that I knew of. and I could only marvel at how he could come up with such marching songs spontaneously. Later that night I persuaded a friend to sneak out of the barracks and go to another PX, buy some candy bars and drink some more beer. He consented even though getting caught would have landed us in serious trouble. Anyway we were successful on this mission and escaped detection. We handed out the candy and the wise ones ate theirs immediately and flushed the wrappers down the toilet. Others were caught in an inspection. I thought I had the perfect hiding place. I was on a lower bunk and put my candy bar between the springs and the mattress. I didn't expect anyone to crawl under the bunk. One night I had a candy bar but was too tired to take the wrapper and flush it down the toilet. Therefore I just stuffed it back under my mattress. In the middle of the night I was awakened by a flashlight in my face. It was one of our sergeants and he was obviously angry. He ordered me to get out of bed and stand at attention. He was holding my candy wrapper which must have fallen out on the floor. He asked "what is this?:" I replied that it was a candy bar wrapper but I didn't know where it came from. He threw my mattress on the floor. Luckily this had been my last candy bar. He then simply said "I'm going to get you for this." Time went by and I began thinking that he had forgotten about the incident. As it turned out he did get me one day before just before we were about to have lunch. First he had me do push-ups until I couldn't do any more. Then he had me low crawl through a long stretch of gravel. He made me do some more things that were aimed just at humiliation and I won't describe these. Anyway when he finally let up I was almost in tears. He made me serve the CO's table at which he too was sitting. As I served that sergeant I had a thought about kicking him in the face. It would have been so easy and I came so close to doing it that it was frightening. At the time I didn't even think about the consequences...When the sergeant told the CO of what I had done the CO asked to see my PT (physical training) scores. As it turned out I had scored 490 out of a possible 500 and was tied for first place in the company. The CO remarked that without the candy bar I could have made 500. I almost laughed at this but quickly realized that this would not be a good idea. Later when we were working in the field with our rifles the sergeant was ahead of us and off to the side. A target appeared and I shot it. The sergeant casually stepped behind some trees. I think he was afraid I might shoot him.

When we finished basic training we were allowed to have a party in a large building on the beach. Parents were also invited. Needless to say we all got drunk. At one time a friend approached me and said "Why are you leaning on my mother?". I suspect that I was telling her about how bad basic training was and then dozed off on her shoulder.

Some days earlier our CO had announced where each of us going for Advanced Individual Training and what our MOS would be. (MOS meaning specialty). We had already had tests that were supposed to determine where we would be most valuable. I had dreams of just being a clerk so I wouldn't have to struggle through the jungles and wait for a VC to shoot me. I had already taken a typing test and done very well.

I also took a German test because I was quite fluent in that language due to my mission. However, when our MOS's were announced I was to be a combat engineer. This, as the saying went, meant that you carried a shovel as well as a rifle. On my aptitude test I answered questions in the way a prospective clerk would. For example if the test asked you whether you liked the great outdoors and adventure. as opposed to working in a dingy office doing boring work I would select the dingy office. I also made it clear that I didn't know anything about firearms. I couldn't even guess which end was the muzzle. Obviously the army didn't pay any attention to our aptitude tests. My last hope was that I would end up in Germany where some other troops were going. My AIT training was held at Fort Leonard, Missouri. While I was there I did little or no drinking—I don't know why. Then came the time when were told where we headed. It was something like this: "Johnson Germany, Jones Germany, Olsen Germany, Jackson Vietnam" As a matter of fact about half of our platoon went to Germany. The fact that I had proven to be fluent in German was thus ignored. Well—that's the army for you. The guys that were going to Vietnam were given some jungle training and had to sleep in the field for a couple of nights. One night the temperature dropped to—7 degrees F.—some jungle training.

We finished our AIT training just before Christmas and were given a one month leave. During that month I did nothing but party. I had resigned myself to death in Vietnam and wanted to squeeze as much fun out of life as I possibly could. I had a girl friend before I was inducted into the army. She didn't drink and didn't appreciate my drinking so I just stayed away from her while I was on my leave. At one time she had made the statement : "It's either me or the bottle". I had immediately grabbed my bottle and had a swig. This angered her so much that she insisted upon going home from the drive-in movie. After that I didn't call for about for a month. When I did call we made a deal that I would never again drink while in her presence. She didn't try to push me into saying something like "I'll never drink again". At any rate I had to make up something to explain why I hadn't called her earlier while on my leave. I told her that I had just arrived home the day before and had a lot of things to do and that I only had a week at home. I took her out once and then spent part of my last evening with her. I told her that I had to go home and pack even though I had already packed. Notice how alcohol makes us lie. I just went over to my friends' house and pro-ceeded to get blitzed. I had to get up early the next day and I had a severe hangover. There were quite a few people at the airport to see me off. I attributed this to the fact that they probably thought they would never see me again. When the plane left I had a sinking feel-ing in my stomach.

We were first taken to Travis Airforce base. We stayed there for about a week before we could get a flight to Vietnam. I did no drinking whatsoever during that week. I was very dejected and feeling sorry for myself. I finally called my girl friend and asked her to marry me if I were somehow not killed. We did get to watch the Super Bowl which matched up John Unitus and Joe Namath. After about a week we finally were boarded on a flight. The plane was not a military plane but just a regular commercial airliner plane with stewardesses and so forth. Our first stop was in Hawaii at Hickam field. We couldn't believe how warm it was. I can't even remember what I did with the heavy coat I was wearing out to the airport. I suspect I must have given it to my parents before I boarded the plane. After Hawaii our next stop was Guam, and then Yokahama (or something like that) in Japan. From there we flew to Vietnam and landed at the Long Binh airport. I was amazed that any airline would land in Vietnam but the stewardess' all wished us luck and promised that they would pray for us.

We were housed at Long Binh for about a week where we underwent a jungle training course.(No—7 degree temperature this time)—We were free to drink in the evenings so of course I took advantage of that. Finally we were given our orders as to where we to be stationed. I was stationed at Dong Tam which was a large base down in the Mekong delta and about 60 miles (or maybe kilometers south of Saigon). At first I was to be a minesweeper then somebody's mind changed and I was instead placed in a bridge building company. I was quite relieved as I didn't relish the idea of being blown up by a mine. As a bridge builder I only had to go into the field perhaps three or four times. On these missions we only built one pontoon bridge. The rest of the missions were a matter of salvaging what we could from the bridges the VC had blown up.

On one occasion we did come under fire and it scared me to death. A guy right next to me was shot. I got a glimpse of someone in the bushes across the river where the fire had come from. I took a couple of quick shots at him but am not sure whether I hit him or not. This was pretty much all of the fighting I did. The only other thing I had to worry about were mortar rounds and rockets We had bunkers that would stop the mortar rounds but possibly not the rockets. Not too long after I arrived there the Tet offensive began. It was not as bad as the as the 68 Tet offensive but it was certainly bad enough for me. We slept in the bunkers and listened to the sound of mortars coming closer and closer.

I've digressed much more than I intended so let's get back to the basic issue. Upon my arrival word had somehow gotten around that I was a Mormon. Upon being asked I replied that I was but was not an active Mormon. I was asked if I drank and I replied in the affirmative. Then some of the guys produced a couple of fifths and we went to work on them. I'm sure they were trying to drink me under the table but they were unsuccessful. Finally the guy who had started the whole thing suggested that we go out to the bunker because he had something special for us. He produced a pipe and loaded it with something. I think it was just marijuana but it might have been what they call hashish. The pipe was passed around and I can't remember what happened after that. I woke up in the morning lying in the dust on a much traveled. dirt road. I remember that the dust was even in my mouth. I struggled to my feet and made it back to my barracks where I took a shower and got dressed just as everyone else was getting up. By that time I wasn't feeling too bad and I even managed to eat breakfast.

It seemed like every night was a party. One of the guys had a refrigerator which he always kept stocked with beer. If we wanted hard stuff (we couldn't buy it ourselves) we knew a lieutenant who, for a small fee would get us anything we wanted. As I said, every night was a party and it seemed like everyone got high in some manner or another. Some guys took pills, some smoked grass, some just drank like I did. We even had a few glue sniffers who would gather together with their little bags. I once saw a guy drinking aqua-velva aftershave. I told him that this was very dangerous but he replied that he did it all the time.

Paydays were always interesting as a drunken poker game would break out. Many guys lost their entire monthly pay in one night. Fights always broke out and there was constant bickering. I played in a couple of games but was too cheap to bet high or even to stay in a high stakes game. Besides I was trying to save up enough to buy a Camaro after my army tour. There was one guy who always seemed to win. He was our Jewish company clerk. He had so much money that he began lending it out with a steep interest rate. His main customers were some of the guys who had blown their whole monthly paychecks in poker games. We all thought the clerk was cheating somehow but we could never catch him doing it.

As for drinking for the most part I confined myself to beer except on two occasions. I developed an interest in history and spent quite a lot of time at our little library. We also had a service club which sold beer and had pretty young Vietnamese girls as waitresses You could offer any of these $5 and be taken care of. This was one activity that I managed to avoid, I was simply too scared of contracting a venereal disease. Every morning someone would go on sick call and we all knew that it was another case of gonorrhea. Some even bragged about how many times they had gotten the "clap" as we called it.

After about 3 months my dream came true and I became a clerk. My predecessor was a very heavy drinker and drank only hard stuff. I suspect that he also had some mental problems. At any rate he was sent stateside. I remember going out one morning and finding him at the bottom of the stairs that led up to the top story of the barracks. He had a bloody nose and seemed to be unconscious. I managed to wake him up and asked him what had happened. He couldn't remember so I just assumed that he had fallen down the stairs. I managed to get him up and more or less carried him up the stairs. I practically had to undress him but I finally managed to get him in the shower. On that particular day we were to go to the rifle range and sight in our M-16s. I will refer to the guy I helped as Joe. I advised him to go on sick call but he said he felt alright. As it turned out he was not alright. He couldn't hit the target let alone the bulls eye. Finally Joe switched his rifle to full automatic and began shooting at all the targets. Needless to say he was in big trouble. It was not long after that he was sent stateside. He needed a replacement and about 5 of us applied for the job. It was no contest. A few of them could hardly read or write. My job as a PLL clerk was to maintain an inventory of trunk parts and order things as necessary. I also had to maintain a log for each truck and there were dozens of them.

At one time we were to have an inspection from some high ranking officers the next day. My records were not quite up to date and I worked feverishly to get them right. That morning I took my log book and walked through the motor pool to ensure I hadn't missed anything. To my horror I found a truck that wasn't even listed in my records. I didn't have time to go through the process of creating a new record as all kinds of information was required as well as a log book entry for any repair information. I probably could have done this but it would have taken all night. Finally I went back to the barracks and went to bed hoping that the inspectors would somehow miss my problem. From what I was told they would do essentially do the same thing that I had done. They would select some vehicles at random and then require me to produce the records for that vehicle. I figured the chances were slim that my recordless vehicle would be picked. That night we had a serious mortar attack and some of the rounds hit in the motor pool. I almost prayed that my little office would be hit and my records destroyed or that the recordless truck would be hit. The next morning we went out to the motor pool to inspect the damage. God must move in mysterious ways because my truck had indeed been hit and nearly destroyed. They hauled it off someplace along with several others and we were then ready for inspection. I passed with flying colors and was even complimented. Needless to say I was very relieved. Some of the guys must have thought I was out of my mind when I saw my truck's condition and began cheering the for the Viet Cong.

As a clerk I never had to leave the base except one time to drive to Saigon with another guy and get steaks for our regular drunken Sunday barbeques. We were fired upon during the journey and we heard the shots screaming by. We were okay but we got the hell out of there as quick as we could. The closest call I had aside from the attack I mentioned earlier, was from a GI who had gone berserk and started shooting all over the place. It was night but I was working in my little office to bring some records up to date. Suddenly bullets began crashing through the thin wall. I laid down and just stayed there wondering if the VC had overrun the base. I didn't even have my M-16. Soon I heard voices and went outside where I found out what had happened.

One night when we were all drunk we were ordered to go out to the berm that surrounded our base because Intelligence suspected that the VC might try to overrun the base that night. Our sergeant, who was probably drunker than any of us began yelling at us to get a truck, etc. We got the truck, loaded up and took off. Our sergeant was standing at the back of the truck and when the driver shifted gears he fell out. We all looked at each other and laughed while he was yelling for us to stop. We pretended not to hear him and said afterward that we were not even aware that he had fallen from the truck. He wasn't about to press any charges because of the embarrassment that he would experience if he admitted to falling out of a truck. Incidentally there was no attack. That's our military intelligence—a true oxymoron.

After I had been in Vietnam for 9 or 10 months we were part of Nixon's first pullout, As we were packing the guys were sneaking in little bags of marijuana, etc. Dogs found most or them so we had to a lot of unloading and then loading again. We were on our way to Hawaii and the guys didn't know if we would have a source there. I might also mention that we were subjected to periodic "shakedown" inspections where our CO would go through all lockers, etc. The company clerk, probably prompted by our CO, would tell us when one was coming up and the guys would hide anything like grass. My office became filled with little bags which were hidden behind motor pool parts, etc. I didn't like this idea but finally agreed just to avoid trouble.

Overall I did pretty good as far as not drinking to excess while I was in Vietnam—I probably averaged a couple of beers per day. There were two occasions where I really got plastered. The first I have already talked about—that was when I tried the hashish after heavy drinking. I might note that I never again tried hashish or marijuana. I simply didn't trust them. I stuck with my reliable beer for the most part. When my 25th birthday arrived the guys got our renegade lieutenant to get us couple of bottles so that we could have a party. I really got blitzed that time as did several others.

Vietnam was quite an experience. I can certainly relate to "MASH" as things were that crazy. None of us had finished our service time and we were actually given a choice as to where we wanted to go to finish our tours. Some chose places near their families but most of us went to Hawaii. In Hawaii we were greeted by a band and were given a huge steak dinner. We were stationed at Schofield Barracks which is kind of in the middle of Oahu. I kept my job as a PLL clerk. I did quite well as far as drinking except for the weekends. I began lifting weights to build up my body. I did this practically every night. Some nights I would stop at the service club and have a cold beer and sometimes not. The weekends were a different story. Regardless of what we planned to do alcohol was always included. There were 3 main places that we went. to on weekends : The first was a small town about 3 miles from the base named Wahiawah. One guy in the company had a car so we sometimes got rides to this town. When we didn't have a ride we would either catch a bus or quite often just walk. Once there we would immediately buy a bottle and proceed to get drunk. Then we would either go to a porno movie or to a bar. When we went to the bar we would almost always find members of our company already there. We would have a good time playing pool and drinking beer. We made friends with a huge Hawaiin man whose name was Tim. One time in the bar we almost got into a fight with some civilians over a pool game. One of the civilians asked me to go outside. I was ready to do so but Tim grabbed me. He then said "I go out with him you, not you.". Needless to say everything settled down. This was the bar in which I became somewhat of a legend. We had talked for some time about trying to steal a beer advertisement that hung on the wall. It was pretty cool with all of its neon lights. I was just drunk enough to try and steal it. First I got my friends car keys. I unlocked his trunk and left it open. I then went back in the bar. The bartender was busy and his back was turned to me so I quickly unplugged the sign and walked out with it, put in my friend's car and then walked nonchalantly back into the bar and started playing pool. It took a while for the bartender to even notice that the sign was missing as there were other signs. As soon as did notice he said "alright what did you guys do with my sign?." We replied that the sign had not been there when we first walked in. After we got back to the barracks we tried to figure out a way to hang our sign on the wall but we were afraid of pounding nails or anything like that. Finally we put it on top of the refrigerator. This was appropriate because there was nothing but beer in the refrigerator. There was even an electrical outlet for the refrigerator so I would plug the sign in at night. I was sure our CO would make me get rid of it he but didn't. He did ask us where we had procured the sign. We replied that we had purchased it—that the owner intended to replace it anyway so he sold it to us cheap. I'm sure our CO didn't believe us but didn't interrogate us anymore. I should mention that I was quite intoxicated when I stole the sign. I would never done it had I been sober. I suppose something like this has happened to all of us alcoholics—we do things when we're drunk that we wouldn't even dream of doing when sober. This was also rather dumb because the bartender was our friend and he might have gotten into trouble. We took the sign back the next weekend.

I began to worry about my friend, Mike, after one of our little trips to this little town.(Wahiawah), We still had some booze left so we brought it back to the barracks. Mike came over and almost begged for a drink. I said "Mike, the party's over. Lets save this for next week.". He explained that he wouldn't be able to sleep without a drink and I finally gave him the bottle. I consider this a sure sign of alcoholism—drinking after the party's over.

The second place that we would go to was the Waikiki Strip. We spent a lot of time at the beeches. During the day we would lay on the beach, suntan and drink. Glass wasn't allowed on the beech so we bought a plastic container that we could fill from our bottle. We would do some swimming and body surfing. Once we rented surf boards and tried to learn surfing. Mike had a terrible time but I was actually getting the hang of it. Of course the waves were pretty gentle—just barely big enough to surf on. We would stay on the beach for most of the day and we ended up with great suntans. It felt rather strange to be laying on the beach on Christmas day. Towards evening we would go eat somewhere and then go to our favorite bar "The Lemon Tree". We would dance and try to arrange dates, etc. Actually we were after only one thing and again I'm sure that you know what that was. We would even prowl the strip hoping to run into some lonely girls. Several times we got lucky and I'm not going into the details. I became even more sure that Mike was an alcoholic based upon what happened in "The Lemon Tree". There were four of us sitting at a table and drinking even though we were already drunk. Mike muttered something about going outside for a minute. When he didn't come back for a while we decided to look for him. We found him sound asleep on his back and was lying crosswise on the sidewalk. The sidewalk was busy and people were just stepping over him. As we watched we saw a few people stop to see if he was alive. His snoring gave them the answer. We got him up and found that he wanted more to drink. We tried to tell him that he'd had enough but he ignored us. We all got so drunk that we didn't want to wait for a bus so we stayed in the apartment of a friend of mine—a guy that I grew up with. I hadn't seenhim for years and it was certainly a strange coincidence that we just happened to run into each other in Hawaii.

One night we decided that we wanted to go to a different bar and we asked a guy if he could recommend a place. He did so and gave us directions. He said that he was certain that we would enjoy it. At first glance it looked great with lots of women and very few guys. Mike almost immediately started dancing but I was just looking around. A couple of girls walked by me and I could hear them talking—in male voices. I looked around some more and it was obvious that some were transvestities. However I wasn't sure about some of them—they appeared to be really nice looking women. I walked around for a few minutes but could hear nothing but male voices. A moment later Mike came off the floor and said "that was a man—I didn't even notice until it said something to me"

I said "Let's get out of here Mike—they're all men!" Some of the transvestites could have passed for women anywhere. Most of them would give themselves away when they spoke but others actually had women-like voices. This made it very difficult for us. We heard a story of a guy from another company had who actually found out the hard way that his girl was a man. He had run his hand up her leg and found something that shouldn't have been there. The story had gotten around so everyone razzed him and made lewd comments. One time we steered a new guy to one of these transvestites. They walked away together so she must have had a woman-like voice. When we ran into the guy later he said "Why didn't you tell me that was a man?" We just laughed and told him that most of us had learned the hard way and that we wouldn't tell on him. Once again we had done something that we wouldn't have done if we had been sober.

It seemed like whenever we went into town we would run into guys from our company. One night it seemed like our whole company was on the Waikiki strip. They were doing the same thing we were—getting drunk and looking for women. Mike and I were sitting on a bench adjacent to the sidewalk. Suddenly a member of our company came racing down he sidewalk. "Help me" he cried as he saw us. Then we saw what he was running from. Closely behind him were four transvestites carrying their high heeled shoes and trying as hard as they could to catch the guy we called Gomer. We were laughing so hard that we couldn't do anything. Finally we got up but laughter left us paralyzed. Later we found out that he had punched. one of the transvestites for being a man.

The third place we often went was the North shore and in particular Waimea bay, one of my favorite places on the earth. We were aware that we had seen the bay on TV as well as nearby Sunset Beach whenever big surfing tournaments were televised. One day we rented surfboards and drove to the North Shore and Waimea bay. We figured we needed to move on since we had conquered Waikiki.

We noticed immediately that the waves were much bigger than those at Waikkiki. I paddled out and waited for a good wave, Suddenly the waves started getting bigger and bigger until they were about 6 feet high I caught one and managed just barely to stand up. For about 5 seconds I was flying. The next thing I knew I was underwater and being rolled all over the place. The water wouldn't let me up and I was running out of air. I tried to swim up but instead swam down and touched sand. I immediately swam the other way and reached the surface just before I would have had to breathe in some water. My surfboard was headed for shore and I couldn't catch it—not that I was going to use it for anything but a floatation device. I was so exhausted from my wipeout that I could I could barely make it to shore The guys told me that when I wiped out my board sailed about 20 feet in the air. From that time on I confined my surfboarding to Waikiki beach.

We did body surf when the waves weren't: too big. That was a lot of fun. I should mention that we always had liquor and beer with us when we went to the beech.

One day we heard on the news that there was a big storm at sea and it would probably result in waves as high as 60 feet on the north shore. Of course we got in our friends Corvair. We had a bottle of rum and finished it off by the time we got to the north shore. The waves were indeed huge. We went first to Sunset beach. There was a big rock out about 40 feet and we were trying to run out when the water was receding and get back before the next wave arrived. This was just plain stupid and very dangerous. We heard later that a couple of Navy guys were playing games like ours and they both drowned. Suddenly we saw a gigantic wave coming in and could see that it was going to get us so we hung onto palm trees. The wave did indeed hit us and it was very hard to hang on especially when the water receded. and almost tore me from my palm tree. We decided that we'd better get out of there and went to get our shoes and socks but couldn't find them. Apparently the wave had claimed them. Anyway we all walked barefooted back to the car and got in. Just then a monster of a wave came in and washed us across the parking lot. We didn't think the car would start but it did and we started back to the barracks. When we came to a place where a Hawiian waved for us to stop. We did and he told us that a big one was coming. We looked out and didn't see anything big enough to hit the road. Therefore we resumed driving and as the road turned toward the beech. I suddenly saw a huge wave towering over us. I barely got the passenger window up before the wave hit us. It washed us right across the road and into a little gully. This time the car wouldn't start for quite a while. Fortunately no more of these huge waves came in and we finally got the car started. It took 4 of us to muscle it back on the road.

Mike outdid himself on one Saturday. We were having a barbeque at the motor pool. Of course we had beer and Mike was feeling no pain. There was an armored vehicle bridge launcher (much like a tank) and Mike had never driven one before. For that matter neither had I. Mike suggested that we take it for a little spin. I tried to talk him out of it because I knew we'd get into trouble. He finally said that he was going to drive it anyway and he did so without yours truly. Somehow he lost control and crashed right through a cinder block wall—a wall of the motor pool bay. Obviously he got into real trouble and he was even told that he would have to pay for the wall. Of course he didn't really have to pay but he was afraid for a while.

I actually knocked off 3 months from my tour of duty by enrolling in my former college for summer quarter. You could do this but it required a letter from the school. A friend of mine had done the same thing and gotten an early out. We were drafted at the same time and thus released at the same time, both of us getting early outs for school. We landed in Seattle. Nobody spit on us but there were a bunch of hippy types that were calking us baby-killers. My friend wanted to fight them all and I had a hard time restraining him especially since I wanted to fight too. I told him that we would get into trouble unless we could get them to throw a punch. My friend called them every name in the book and more but they wouldn't take the bait. An airport security guard then stepped in and dispersed the hippies. He commented that he hated them but is was his job to break up any fights and to defuse any potential ones. It took several days to get a flight to Salt Lake City where we both were going. Fortunately the airport had sleeping quarters just for GIs. Finally we got a flight and soon we were home.

It was time to pick up our lives again and not have to worry about mortars, etc. I still flinch when I hear a loud noise like a car backfiring. As far as picking up life I pretty much picked mine up where I'd left off—going to school, working part-time and drinking as well as chasing women. As I have mentioned I had enrolled for summer quarter. I changed my major from chemical engineering to history due to the interest that I had developed in history in Vietnam. It was now 1970. While I was taking my last final I saw my car drive up. My sweet Camaro convertible was already packed for a trip to New Orleans. My friends got out and to get my attention knocked on the window then motioned for me to come out. The professor went out and shooed them away. They came back and were even worse. I knew that I wouldn't be able to concentrate so I simply turned in my incomplete final and walked out. I did manage to pass the class despite my incomplete final exam.

We had a lot of fun on the trip and drank a lot of booze. In Colorado we were pulled over by a highway patrolman. As soon as we heard the siren Bob sprayed his mouth with some breath freshener. We were all equipped with these aerosol breath fresheners just in case of an incident like this. The patrolmen came up to the car and told us that the inside lane was only to be used for passing. Bob handled himself well and quickly we were on our way again. Another time I was driving and a guy in a corvette apparently wanted to race me. I knew his car was more powerful than mine but I got up to 120 mph and then began to slow down till I was at 70 mph which was fast enough for me. It was then that we heard a siren behind us so we pulled over. To our surprise the highway patrol car went right past us. He was apparently after the corvette. Sure enough after several miles we saw the corvette and the patrol car As we neared the officer motioned for us to pull over. I quickly used my mouth spray while he wasn't looking. He was writing out a ticket for the corvette driver. After he had finished with the other guy he came over to our car. He told us that we had been speeding too but he just gave us a warning ticket. Fortunately he must have clocked us after I slowed down. After that we were careful not to exceed the speed limit. It would be just too easy to get a drunken driver charge.

In Kansas one morning we ran out of gas. We had thought we could make the next town so hadn't filled up in the previous one. We were getting ready for a long walk when Steve suggested that we walk down to a little house and see if the owner happened to have a can of gas that we could buy. A man answered the door and we asked him where the nearest gas station was. He said "right here". Then we saw that he had his own pump. He filled a can for us and told us to get the car started and drive back to the pump. He filled up my car but refused to take any money. About that time his wife came out and said that breakfast was ready and she insisted that we eat with them. This really restored my faith in humanity.

We finally reached Bossier city which was near New Orleans. We spent the night there but first went to a bar where we met some girls. The next day we drove into New Orleans. First of all we got a motel room and then went to see the sights. We actually stayed sober in New Orleans for the most part. We did get thrown out of one bar because Steve threw a wiffle ball at a stripper. He had found the wiffle ball out on the sidewalk and still had it when we went into the bar. We asked him why he had thrown it and he replied that he had just felt like it. After staying several day in New Orleans we started the long trip home We did some drinking on the way but not really that much.

When we got back I resumed my old life—college, part time work and drinking on the weekends. As before we would try to meet girls mostly by dancing with them in bars. On one of these nights in at our favorite bar I noticed a little redhead who was really cute. She was sitting with a rather handsome guy but he looked somewhat feminine. I pointed her our to my two friends and they challenged me to ask her to dance. I wasn't afraid of the guy because of the fact that I was pretty built up from my weight lifting in Hawaii. At any rate I finally asked the girl to dance. She said yes and the guy didn't say anything. When I asked her about him she told him that he was just a friend. The girl gave me her phone number and I called her on Monday. We arranged a date for the next weekend and had a good time. From that time on I stopped trying to meet other girls and took my little redhead out every weekend. It wasn't long until I was seeing her every night. I did a lot off drinking at her home. Every time I went to her house her parents would tell me to fix myself a drink. I would do that and make very strong drinks. A few months after I met this Katie, spring quarter at my college was commencing and she also took some classes there. We would always meet when we had some free time. Normally Katie didn't drink except when we went to a dancing bar. On the other hand I would drink regardless of what we were doing. One night she asked my why I always had to drink when we went out. I can't remember how I responded but I did stop drinking when I was with her unless she was drinking too. As I said we were both enrolled at the University of Utah for spring quarter but Katie changed to a private college, because she thought they had a better program for nurses.

I graduated from the University of Utah in 1972 with a degree in history. I had intended to teach but there were no positions open. I even took a civil service exam and scored very high. However the only job I was offered was as a tax auditor and I didn't want to do that. Since I had the GI Bill to pay my tuition I decided to go to the community college and study something more practical. Computers were big at the time and I figured I wouldn't have any problem finding a job after I graduated. For the next two years I spent my time on college, part time work, Katie and drinking. My drinking was getting worse but I still don't think I was an alcoholic—I was certainly a problem drinker.

I started out well enough in the Community college but my drinking became worse. I was drinking practically every night. I just about always missed my 7:30 A.M class. However my brother was in the class and would give me the assignments and I did pass. As my brother and I made friends we started to party together. We all finished by 1:00 P.M. and then we would go to a bar named "The Red Devil. There we would play pool, pinball. and mainly drink. It got to the point where we were going almost every day. However when I got low on money I would take a week off from "The Red Devil" and work, One day a guy I will call John had to leave early for a dental appointment. We all left shortly after that. My brother and I were in my Volkswagen. I can't recall where we were going but I had to urinate. We drove down a little alley and found a good place for me. As we continued down the alley we saw a tombstone leaning against a fence. It had no inscription on it so we loaded it into my car for some reason. Then we decided to leave it on John's porch as a joke. It was heavy enough that it required two people to carry it. After that we didn't see John for about two weeks. When we asked him where he had been he told us that he had been in Wyoming. He said that he had become somehow involved with some "bad" guys and that he owed them some money. He figured that the tombstone was a threat from them. After spending almost two weeks he managed to get in touch with a member of the ring and was told that they didn't know anything about the tombstone. Once he had found that out he returned to Salt Lake City. Now he wanted to find out who had put the stone on his porch. My brother and I confessed and expected John to be very angry. Instead he just laughed the whole thing off. Once again we did something that we never would have done if we had been sober. My brother and I felt very bad about the whole thing. We had, in fact, wasted two weeks of John's life.

John was quite a character. One day he told us that he had been stopped by the highway patrol on the freeway. He was trying to be very careful because he was quite drunk. The patrolman asked if he knew how fast he was going. John replied that he was certainly not speeding. "No kidding" said the officer. "You were going 15" John then said that there was something wrong with the car and that was as fast as it could go. The officer then told him to get off the freeway.... My weekends were spent with Katie. Often we would go to a private club where we would drink and dance. Katie would get plowed once in a while but normally she would just have a couple of drinks. I, on the other hand, would always get at least semi-drunk.

Drinks in the club were very expensive so I started bringing my own bottle. Of course I couldn't. take my bottle into the club so I did the next best thing. I would buy a drink or two and then nurse the last one throughout the night. Whenever I wanted a real drink I would go out to my car and take a few hits from my bottle of vodka.

Finally graduation time rolled around and we were required not only to attend but to wear cap and gown. Our little club met an hour before the graduation ceremony at "The Red Devil" and we consumed as much beer as we could before going to the ceremony.

After graduating I got a one room apartment. I hired on as a computer operator at a large corporation on July 1, 1974. I was promised that I would soon be promoted to a programming position. On August 30 Kate and I were married. We had some problems finding a priest that would marry us since I was Mormon and Cathy was Catholic. Finally we found one who would marry us as long as I promised that I wouldn't interfere with Cathy's attempts to raise our future children as Catholic. This didn't really bother me because I believed that as our children grew older, they would make up their own minds. At the reception I got quite drunk. We stayed in a downtown luxury hotel and what happened was a result of my drinking. I was smoking in bed and apparently dropped an ash between the bed frame and the mattress. We went to sleep but shortly my new wife woke me saying that she could smell smoke. I could tell that is was the mattress and began throwing water on it using the ice container. It was to no avail as the mattress kept smoldering. Soon the smoke was so bad that I sent my wife out into the hall. in her robe. I will never forget seeing her sitting in the hallway crying and holding her wedding dress, I quickly dialed 911 and then made my own exit as the smoke was just too much for me. I seemed to smell the smoke for several days and so did my wife. The firemen soon arrived but had a difficult time getting the fire out. Katie and I went back to our apartment. In the morning we left for our honeymoon and were in amazingly good spirits. We were even joking about the whole thing. I might note that we got a bill from the hotel in the amount of some $250. We never paid it as we knew they had insurance and we never heard from them again. For our honeymoon we went up to Jackson Hole and then through Yellowstone Park. We had a lot of fun but I also drank a lot, My wife complained about my drinking so for the rest of the honeymoon I didn't drink.

After we got home I resumed work and Katie continued college, now at a private institution. We were actually living on the 3 dollars per hour the I made. For a time I tried to hold down most of two jobs. My shift at the computer corporation started at 2:00 A.M. and ended at 10:00 A.M. I would sleep for a couple of hours and then go to work for four more hours at my old part time job. This schedule didn't last long because I just couldn't take it. Probably the only good thing, aside from the money was the fact that there was no longer any time at all for drinking. I would drink a couple of beers on occasion. After three weeks I quit my part-time job. I could still work there whenever I wanted but I only did this a few times. Now I had only one job and a crazy shift but I did have some available time for drinking and I took advantage of it.

I would normally arrive home at about 10:30 A.M. Instead of immediately going to bed I would stay up and drink until about 1:00 P.M., often without even eating and then get in bed. I would get up at about 6:00 P.M. and immediately fix a drink. My wife was still in school so she knew nothing of my morning drinking. I tried to be back in bed by 10:00 P.M. but seldom made it. I was getting enough sleep but it wasn't good sleep due to the alcohol. I was always tired. Monday mornings were particularly difficult as my wife and I had a group of friends that would go to a bar on Sunday nights where they played only "oldies" and we wouldn't leave until after midnight. I would just have time to shower and get to work. On one morning a colleague remarked that I smelled like a brewery. The next week I put on cologne and had some breath mints. He then he told me that I smelled like a French whore. I tried to limit my drinking on Sunday nights but was never very successful. Finally our "Bongo Lounge" nights became just too much for me even though I would take a long nap on Sunday afternoons. For the next 9 months I worked and my wife went to school. I kept the same shift during that time and finally got used to it. I managed to get my drinking in. After getting off work at 10:00 A.M. I would usually stop at the liquor store. When the employees go to know me by name I switched to another liquor store. I was actually afraid to buy more than a pint at a time because I knew what I would do. Eventually I began buying half-gallons and stashing them somewhere that my wife wouldn't be likely to look. However that was a few decades later and I'll write about it when I get to that part of my life.

As mentioned I was a computer operator for 9 months and was then assigned to a project and promoted to assistant programmer or something like that. I never really knew or cared what my job title was. I just cared about the money. I never did have any desire to get into management even though the opportunities were there. Perhaps if I hadn't been an alcoholic I might have pursued a management position but I doubt it. I know of others who were well qualified to be managers but they would rather "get down in the trenches" with the troops. My brother is a manager at another computer company and has told be a lot of horror stories as far as handling employees, etc.

My hourly rate went from $3 per hour to $33 during that 27 year period. In retrospect we were almost as well off when I was making $3 per hour as we are now very deeply in debt. I just realized that I have just given away the fact that my wife has somehow remained with me. Why she stayed is far beyond me as she had every right and justification to divorce me. The only real fights we had were over my drinking. I might mention that today, August 30, we are celebrating our 30th anniversary.

It's time to get back to the story. We left off at the point where I had been assigned to a project. I hoped to write software but instead was put in charge of all the record keeping and making releases to the customer. This proved to be very difficult and complicated but I managed to do a good job despite the fact that I was now drinking almost every night.

At any rate I was a computer operator from July 1974 to March 1975. From March 1975 to March 1976 I was on a project as some kind of a programmer. In March the manager of the project called everyone together. It was not a formal meeting as he just herded everyone into one aisle. He told us that the project had been cancelled and basically everyone on the project was to be laid off. Then he said they were bringing in interviewers from other corporation sites. He said that he thought we would all get jobs although relocation might be necessary. Some of the programmers were able to find jobs with other projects in Salt Lake City. However I didn't know any of these managers nor did they know me. The local jobs went almost exclusively to the people who had been around a long time and knew everybody.

We were then told that we all had a week off and then the interviewers would be there. I was so shocked that I kept on working for a while. Then I finally realized there was nothing to work for. Everyone was taking their personal property home—things like pictures, plants, etc., so I began to do the same. For the rest of that week I remained pretty well drunk. On the day before the interviewers were to be there I didn't drink as I wanted to be as sharp as I could the next day. The next day arrived and job seeders started trickling in. I got there early just because I hoped, ridiculously, that I would be hired on the spot before others got interviewed. I talked to several interviewers but they wanted specialized skills that I didn't possess. Finally I talked to a guy from Eagan, Minnesota. After I told him what I had been working on he told me that they did have an opening for me. I told him that I would have to talk with my wife first. He agreed to hold the job for me until the next day. That night Katie and I went to a lounge, ordered drinks and talked the whole thing out. There were only two choices:: take the offer and relocate or reject the offer and try and find a local job. Since local jobs were scarce at the time we finally decided to accept the offer as we really didn't have much choice. In retrospect I think both of us were viewing the thing as an adventure. I was surprised that Katie would consider relocating because she was very close to her parents and sisters. In fact she made a point of calling them every night and we ate with them at least twice a week. I was also close to my parents as well as my 4 sisters and one brother. However I had experienced this type of separation twice—my mission and my tour of duty in the army which totaled four and a half years. Also I had lived for some 6 months with 3 friends in an apartment. Katie, on the other hand, had never really been away from her family for any length of time. She started her college at Utah State which was some 90 miles from Salt Lake City. Even then she would drive home on weekends. One problem with the relocation was the fact that Katie still had a part of a semester to complete and another one after the summer. She planned to fly to Minnesota and stay with me for the summer. At the first of 1997 she would join me for good. This meant I would have to drive the 1200 miles alone in a slow Volkswagen Thing but this didn't bother me. I might add that the Eagan plant was paying for our moving expenses. I drank right up until the day I had to leave. When the movers arrived they went crazy. I didn't know this until later but they had actually packed an empty bottle of vodka and an ashtray that was full of ashes. They were certainly thorough is all I can say. I just sat back on the couch and watched them, vodka collins in hand. They would have packed my full bottle but when I saw them grabbing everything in sight, I took the bottle out to the car. One of them drank one of the beers I had in the refrigerator but I didn't say anything to him as I would have offered it to him had I known he wanted it. Also he was a very big Tongan. He was tearing off strips of wrapping tape whereas the others were using scissors. The next morning I left but I was not alone. My younger brother accompanied me. He was to drive out with me in case I had any problems and then fly back. I know that Mom and Dad were responsible for this although I'm sure my brother would have done it of his own volition had I asked him. It was certainly a long drive but we took turns driving which made it easier. I had a bottle with me and my brother l and I both imbibed quite a bit. I can't remember where we stayed the first night but on the second night we reached Eagan and stopped at the first motel we encountered. My brother had stopped drinking but I still wanted more. The next day I got him on an airplane. I then got a much better room in a hotel that been recommend by the interviewer. There were three us that went to Eagan and I found the other two at that hotel. The company was still footing the bill for the hotel rooms and they did so until we could find suitable apartments.

I found a nice two bedroom in a complex called High Site that was a bit expensive but I expected a raise soon. We had already gotten a 10% bonus for relocating. One big advantage was that the plant where we were to work was right across the street from our apartments—thus no commute was required, The raise I did receive just about doubled what I was making and that was certainly welcome.

Katie was staying at her parents while she finished up school. She called about 3 or 4 times a week so I can't imagine what her parents phone bill must have been. On the nights when she planned to call I would hold off my drinking until she had called. However she called once unexpectedly on a Saturday and that was my big drinking day. I was pretty well plowed and she, of course, asked me if I had been drinking. I of course lied.—"just a couple of beers" I said. I'm sure she knew better but she didn't press the the issue. She has an uncanny way of just hearing my voice or looking in my eyes even when I have just had a couple of beers and determining whether I been drinking. Based upon what I have heard and seen, alcoholics will always lie about their drinking. I certainly did and many times. On Saturdays I would always get a pint for the day and then try to dry out on Sunday for the work week. I had some very brutal Sundays and would usually go and at least get some beer. Then I discovered that a liquor store was open in Hudson, Wisconsin on Sundays. After that I would still try to not drink on Sunday but always seemed to be driving to Hudson to get a bottle. At this point I knew that I had a real problem. I drank after parties, drank alone and would drive to Hudson every Sunday to get a pint to quash my hangover.

You may recall that at the first of the book these are the very factors I listed that indicate that you are an alcoholic. With nobody to discourage me I drank every night. The one thing I will say is that I never drank before work or during the work day. However I would sometimes call in sick when the hangover was especially bad. I was what they term a "functional" alcoholic. I could normally get through a day without drinking and do a good job for my employer but would always drink in the evening.

In September I flew home for my brothers wedding. The wedding was nice and I got a few days with Katie—days when I didn't drink anything. She said she was proud of me and to keep it up when I got back to Minnesota. Needless to say I didn't keep it up. As soon as the plane reached cruising altitude and the seatbelt sign was turned off I ordered a drink and had two more en route to Minnesota. When I arrived at my apartment I had a few more drinks before I went to bed. I continued much the same as I waited for the summer and Katie. I was certainly glad to see her when she came in around the first part of June. Once she was there I tried hard to control my drinking but just couldn't quite do it. Often I would make it for a day or two but then I'd revert to my old ways. We still managed to have a good summer. We did a lot of sightseeing, swimming in the apartment pool and fishing. On either Friday or Saturday we would go over to Fred and Cheryl's and play cards and other games. Fred was one of the guys from Salt Lake City who had also transferred to Eagan. He would make a drink for me and that was all I got but Fred also had only one. Obviously he didn't have the alcohol problem that I did. He seemed to get as high on one drink as I would after six. Finally I began bringing my own bottle and mixing my drinks very strong. I offered drinks to everyone else and then Fred would sometimes have two. My wife would usually have just one as did Cheryl.

I didn't drink that much for a while as I didn't know my job well enough. to go in with a hangover. I got on a softball team and we won the championship. I would have a snort of vodka before the game and after the game we would sit around and drink beer. In July my sister and her husband came to stay with us for a week. We had the two bedrooms so they had a place to stay. My sister's husband was quite a drinker and my sister also imbibed. This made it easy for me to drink. We did a lot of fun however.

At the end of summer Katie had to return to Salt Lake City for her last semester. I was sorry to see her leave but was somewhat comforted by the fact that I would least be able to drink as I pleased without trying to hide anything. The rest of 1976 was uneventful. I worked, drank and watched TV. By November it began to get pretty cold and December was much worse. However I had to drive to get Katie as she had graduated with a four year degree in Nursing. I drove 24 hours straight with just a couple of breaks. Once I started to hallucinate and saw cows on the road. I knew they weren't real cows. They looked very strange and had red eyes. One of them was standing up on its back legs. I stopped at the next rest stop and parked on the side. I kept the car running for the sake of the heater and then began to doze off. Suddenly I heard something. When. I opened by eyes all I could see were red lights. I immediately slammed on the brakes. I thought I had gone to sleep while driving and was about to rear—end someone. Then I realized that I was not moving and neither was the truck in front of me. The truck driver had just pulled in ahead of me. This scared me enough that I was wide awake for awhile and managed to reach Rawlins, Wyoming where I got a cheap motel room. I slept for about 4 hours and then drove the 300 miles to Salt Lake City. Katie and I were very happy to see each other and know that we would never be separated again except for short periods. We stayed in Salt Lake City until New Years Day and I did quite a lot of drinking.

On New Years Day of 1977 Katie and I began our journey back to Minnesota. I don't remember where we stayed the first night. I think it might have been Casper, Wyoming. On the second day we were cruising along pretty well when out gasoline heater went out. I looked at it but could see nothing wrong. We needed to find some-place to stay as the temperature was—10 F. Nightfall came and it got even colder. We were scraping the inside of the windshield. We hadn't even brought a map and we had no idea where the next town was. I was beginning to worry and Katie was beginning to cry.

Finally we hit a little Town called Kadoka. We were in South Dakota at the time. Kadoka even had a motel. We checked in. Katie got in a hot bath while I went to a service station to see if anyone could help us. They did have a mechanic but he just looked at the heater and said he didn't know anything about them. He told us that there was a Volkswagen dealership in Sioux Falls but that was quite a distance.

The next morning we started out and stopped at every place where we could get warm. Finally we got to Sioux Falls and found the Volkswagen dealership. We walked across the street to get something to eat at a restaurant and especially some hot coffee. When we got back the dealership we were told the car was ready. We asked the guy how much we owed him. He said we owed him nothing and he walked over the car. He raised the hood and then had me stick my hand under the heater. I couldn't see it but I felt a switch." That's just a cutoff switch like a circuit breaker" he said "but the owner's manual doesn't even mention that the switch is there.". Once again my faith in humanity was restored as the guy could have charged whatever he felt like and I wouldn't have known the difference. Anyway we now had heat and that made the last leg of journey bearable. When we got home I immediately opened a bottle of vodka and made a drink—my wife even had one too. The next day I went to work and my wife cleaned up and put her clothes and things away.

We had arrived just in time for one the coldest spells in St. Paul's history. For 2 weeks the temperature was never warmer than -30 degrees F. at 7:30 A.M, when we went to work. Once the wind chill factor was included the temperatures were in the -70's. Needless to say we no longer walked even though the plant was only about 2 blocks from my apartment. As a matter of fact there were TV and radio warnings advising people to stay inside if they possibly could, At work people would be going out all day to start their cars. The plant even had 3 or 4 battery chargers that people could use to start their cars.

Fortunately the weather warmed up somewhat in February. Sometime in March a guy called me from the Salt Lake site of the corporation and asked me if I wanted to come back to Salt Lake. Considering the winter we had experienced it was a no-brainer. Another factor for going back was the fact that my wife called her sister and her mother almost every night. Our phone bills were ridiculous. When I told my wife she got all excited and made a bunch of more long distance calls. The trip back was not bad but we did hit a stretch of road between Casper and Rawlins that was very icy. We hit a patch of black ice and immediately did a 360 and ended up out in a field. Fortunately we were able to get the car back on the road without much trouble.

Once we were back in Salt Lake City we rented a two bedroom apartment in the same building that we had previously inhabited. We ended up hating that apartment because it was a basement apartment and was always dark. However we were looking for a house anyway and had not been forced to sign a 6 month lease. We quickly found a house that we liked even though it was under construction. It was only about a mile and one half from Katie's parents home but was in a brand new subdivision. As soon as the house was finished we closed on it and moved in. While we had lived in the depressingly dark apartment I drank a lot. With the new house there were so many things to do that I didn't have much time for drinking. However I still managed to have a beer by my side as I worked.

When we quit for the night I would then drink some hard liquor. Still I was drinking considerably less than I had when we were in the apartment. Thus I learned something—that keeping busy at something really helps with alcohol. My first project was to plant a lawn. My second was to build a good workbench. My third was finishing the basement. I made another bedroom, a family room and a ¾ bathroom. Needless to say, this took a long time. We had decided we would have no children until we had a house. Now we ready to start our family ands Brandon was born on March 3, 1980 and Gary on September 17, 1981. Brandon recently graduated from the University of Washington. Gary got an associate degree from the Community College and now plans to attend Weber State. They are both fine young men and I am very proud of them. I've heard that alcoholism is hereditary. Somehow I don't this will be a problem for my boys since they've seen what torture I've been through.

In 1982 my family had a real crisis. I was trying to fix a screen that my dog had made a hole in but was having a beer at the same time Then I went to one of my "stashed" bottles and had a big drink directly from the bottle I then turned around and saw my wife standing there. She just said "That's it!" and took Brandon to the car and left. I assumed that she had gone to her parents home. Because I was left with Gary I put him on my lap and drove to the liquor store (without a child seat). I took Gary right in the store with me and the clerk even remarked that Gary was a cute child.

While I was doing this I was also detesting myself. I took Gary home along with my bottle My wife shortly drove up and got Gary. I tried to talk to her but she didn't want to talk. I figured the marriage was finished so I just kept on drinking. That night I went over to see Katie and see if I could get her to talk. She said simply that if

I would go to a month-long substance abuse program there might be a reconciliation but if I wouldn't go the marriage was over. I was actually ready to give up on her but when I got home I home I found myself calling my boss and telling him that I wouldn't be in for a month and that I would be in an alcohol abuse program. He said he had never suspected that I had such a. problem but was smart in confronting it before it got any worse. He also said that he could probably get the company to help pay for the treatment. Help indeed! The company paid for everything and the treatment didn't cost me a dime. The treatment itself was a nightmare. First of all you were detoxed if you were still drunk. I wasn't drunk so they just gave me a Librium and sent me to a group discussion, Since I was "the new boy on the block" it seemed like everyone directed their questions and comments to me. I tried to explain that my drinking was erratic and that I could go without alcohol when necessary. Even as I said it I couldn't help but remember my Sunday morning trips to Hudson, Wisconsin. Based upon the criteria I listed earlier they deemed me an alcoholic. I remarked that I was indeed a problem drinker—even a serious problem drinker but that I would be okay if I just summoned up my will-power and decided that I really. wanted to quit drinking. They said that will-power alone wouldn't get the job done. I remembered a story I had heard from my wife. As a nurse she often listened to stories from her patients. On one occasion a patient told her of his drinking and partying in his younger days. My wife asked him if he still drank and he replied that he hadn't had a drink in 30 years. One day had just decided that he was an alcoholic and had to quit drinking. He put his last unopened bottle on top of the refrigerator and never touched it since except to dust it. The bottle still sat on his refrigerator after 30 years and he also had not had a drink in those 30 years.

The guy said he had never been to an AA meeting but had just quit on his own. "If that's not an example of will power defeating alcohol then I don't know what is", I told the group. They replied that this was an exception but not the rule. I replied that if there were exceptions they should be noted and not to always speak in absolutes.

This brings up something that has always bothered me. Alcoholics are people too. They are tied together by one problem—that they are powerless over alcohol. This powerless attribute can manifest itself in many ways. One alcoholic may only go on monthly binges. When he is done with a binge he will be sober for a while until it's time for the next monthly binge. On the other hand alcoholics may drink every day. There are functional alcoholics and dysfunctional alcoholics. I was a functional alcoholic in that I held a good job and did a good job myself. If that were not the case I wouldn't have all the awards and certificates lying around in our study. The simple fact is that I gave the company 27 ½ years of good service. When I came in to work with a hangover I would quickly immerse myself in my work. After several hours my hangover would be gone. The standard statement here is; "but think how much better you could have done without alcohol." I simply don't accept this statement. Some of my best work was done while I was slightly high but not intoxicated. I would never have worked 12—16 hours a day without at least some alcohol. I guess I am just saying that all alcoholics are not alike. In the group conversation I heard statements such as ; "Since you are alcoholic you do this, and this etc," Such talk is nonsense and I refuse to listen to it.

There is only trait that all alcoholics share—the fact that they are powerless over alcohol. This powerlessness can manifest itself in various ways. Also alcoholics do not all act the same when they are intoxicated. One may spout off about something whereas others become more quiet. I expressed this to my counselor and he replied that they didn't have the resources for individual programs and that they were more or less taking a scattergun approach Another problem with the program, at least as I see it, is that all of the counselors. were not at least reformed alcoholics. I think that the only people that can relate to alcoholics is another alcoholic.

I think perhaps the greatest problem for me was that I could not admit that I was powerless over alcohol and that my life had become unmanageable. At any rate I made it through the program and then didn't have a drink for several months. I went to several AA meetings but was never impressed. One guy would talk about his goats getting out. Another lady gave an eloquent polished speech. I went to a different location the next week—the same lady was there and she gave the same speech, almost word for word. This soured me on AA to some extent. I went to an aftercare meeting and found out that a lot of people had slipped. Anyway after several month I started drinking again. I started with a beer or two but soon was drinking as much or more than I had before. I was still a "functional" alcoholic though and that was my rationale for drinking with excuses such as "work is very stressful, etc.". The fact is that one can always find an excuse for drinking, I finished my time at St. Benedicts in October, 1982. During the time I was there my youngest son had learned to walk. I felt bad about this but it didn't deter me long from my drinking. I drank my first hard drink on New Year's Eve, 1982. Once again I was on my way. A couple of years later I actually went for 6 months without a drink. The reasons were two. First I was having some sort of panic attacks and I wanted to if they were in some way related to my drinking. Second I was told that I wouldn't know what sobriety was like until I had gone 6 months without a drink. After the 6 months had gone by I had another panic attack and I was still craving alcohol. In about 1986 my wife and I had a trial separation that lasted for 6 months. I moved into an apartment complex not very from my home. It really wasn't much of a separation. My wife would call me almost every night and if she didn't I'd call her. On Saturdays my wife worked so I got the boys. I would first mow the lawn and then take my two boys back to my apartment. I'd feed them and then take them swimming. All the time I had them I'd be drinking too. I was now drinking more than a pint per day—probably about ¾ of a fifth. I made some friends at the complex and we did a lot of drinking together. After the 6 months were over I moved back into the house. For some years I curtailed my drinking by a huge margin. Finally however, alcohol began to creep up on me again. I made efforts to quit but these lasted for only a week or so and then I'd be right back where I was. By this time our subdivision had become very run down, minorities started moving in and gangs were walking up and down the streets. We were burglarized three times in less than a year. We decided that it was time to move out. We looked around but couldn't find anything that we particularly liked. We did find a model that we did like and decided to have our house built. We sold our old place quite cheaply as we just wanted to get out of there. For the 6 months that our house was being built we lived with my mother who was all alone. I think she really enjoyed our company. Needless to say I greatly cut down on my drinking during those 6 months. We moved into our new home in 1993. Now that we were away from Mom I started drinking more heavily and would cut down only when my wife threatened to divorce me. In 1998 I got my first DUI which cost me $260. This was rather a strange DUI as the arresting officers did not even see me driving. What happened is that I drove into Yellowstone park and immediately stopped at a ranger's shack in order to buy a fishing license. After I had finished and was leaving another ranger walked by and remarked that he could smell alcohol. He at once pointed the finger at me and the next thing I knew I was taking a breath analyzer test. The test showed,091 with the legal limit was,090 We could have said that Katie had been driving the car but I had a big white protector on my nose because I had recently undergone a nose operation. The person at the toll gate would have undoubtedly noticed me. The rangers had me do a bunch of field tests with which I had no trouble but they lied maliciously in their report which I got to hear later. At any rate I had to spend about 6 hours in jail and was then able to leave. About a month later I had to drive up to Mammoth and meet with a judge. It was pretty much a kangaroo court with only myself, the judge and a ranger present. The ranger read off the statement of the arresting officers. Most of the statement was entirely false but there was nothing I could do. The report even stated that I had admitted that I was the driver of the van to three different rangers. The fact is that I only talked to two rangers. The rangers has also told me that the incident would not go on my driving record because it had occurred in a national park. This was another blatant lie. The judge was a pompous jerk. I couldn't even find a way to pay him. He wouldn't take cash nor a credit card and also not a personal check. I ask him what the hell he wanted me to do as these were my only options for payment, He finally agreed to take my check but made some comment about my check being possibly no good. I told him that if he doubted my check just to take the cash. After the whole thing was over and he had taken his robe off he tried to act like a good guy. He asked me how the fishing was and I told him that I hadn't come up to fish.

You might think that this would prevent my drinking and driving but it did so only for a short time. This was rather stupid as I think they revoke your license after the second DUI. According to Utah law I was supposed to have my license suspended for 6 months. However by the time the State Department of Motor Vehicles got the notification the 6 months had already expired. I handed the clerk my driver's license and then $50 and he handed me back my driver's license. For any one watching it must have looked like some kind of a bribe. However the law required me to turn in my driver's license even though I got it back a few seconds later. There were no changes as far as my drinking went for the next few years. I would drink heavily for a while, then even sometimes quit for a week, or at least drink quite lightly. I was actually engaged in some sort of game with my wife. I'd push her until she was about to divorce me and then I'd become sort of a good guy again.

On March 13, 2002 I had a Grand Mal seizure. My mother had died on March 7 and the 6 of us kids had decided to go out and eat before one sister had to return to Switzerland and another to Boston. We were at a Mexican restaurant and I was being bothered by little jerks or spasms. After the meal I just wanted to get home because I just didn't feel right but everyone else wanted to go the cemetery one last time. Katie wanted to go also and, despite feeling very funny, I agreed and we went. At the cemetery I felt alright to begin with. Then as I walking along a sidewalk I felt a big spasm that stopped me in my tracks. I seemed to hear somebody saying "get him down" and that's all I remember. The next thing I remember was waking up and seeing an ambulance and fire truck. I couldn't figure out what was going on and why it had so suddenly become dark. Also why was I on a gurney? Katie told me that I had had a seizure and that she had been afraid she'd lost me. They loaded me into the ambulance and took me to St. Marks hospital. Once we arrived they lifted me onto a hospital bed and pushed me to one side. Some lady started to preach to me about alcohol. I was about to tell her to go away but didn't. I then realized that everyone was assuming that I had had an alcohol-related seizure—due either to withdrawal or overindulging. Neither made sense to me as I had just been having a pretty much normal day—drinking some beer but no hard stuff. They did a cat scan on me and I was told that this ruled out tumors, etc. Anyway they kept me overnight and allowed me to go home the next day. I was referred to a St Mark's neurologist. He wanted an MRI done and also an EGG. The MRI showed nothing and I had to wait one month for the EEG. I didn't drink at all during that month. At any rate I finally had the EEG and it showed abnormal brain activity. For one thing this meant that the seizure was not related to alcohol. The neurologist put me on some anti-seizure medication. The medication was changed several times as some of them caused me to feel dopey and have a hard time speaking. Currently I am taking Lamictal. I was told that I couldn't drink while taking the medication because it would destroy my liver. For about three months I didn't have a drink. However it bothered me to have people tell me that I was "doing good". I would tell them that I hadn't quit drinking but was simply not drinking at the time. As I said I didn't have a drink for 3 months and then we went to West Yellowstone where Brandon was going to participate in a Triatholon. After the triatholon we went into town to get something to eat. While everybody was finishing up I told them that I was going across the street to play a couple of games of video poker. I got a beer and then started to play while watching the street for my family. When I saw that the coast was clear I quickly downed the beer. This one beer started me off again and soon I was drinking vodka just as before. At this time I need to go back to the end of 2001. My company had been downsizing for sometime but thus far I had somehow managed to escape being laid off. In an effort to get rid of people my company added some retirement bonuses for people who were over 55. At first I wasn't interested but found out that the layoff was going to be massive and our group was going to be especially hard-hit. Since I was between projects I knew that I was very vulnerable. I then began to look at the retirement options. The option that I selected would add 3 years to my years of service and 3 years to my age for purposes of calculating pension benefits. It would also provide an extra $500 per month for health insurance until I reached age 65 and was eligible for Medicare. Since I was insured by Katie's health insurance the extra $500 was for us to use as we pleased. As it turned out I would be getting about $1750 net per month. I could have gotten more but I elected for the single annuity option which, in the event of my death, would pay Katie half of my pension. My last day of work was December 31, 2001, As the year 2002 began I began searching for a job. I quickly became discouraged as it appeared that every employer wanted skills that I didn't have. Still I managed to Email my resume to several prospective employers. I didn't hear from them and really became discouraged. I began drinking heavily and this takes us up to the time of my seizure.

As noted I did not drink until about 3 months after the seizure. About one month after the seizure I had an EEG. I did no drinking at all during this month. The EEG showed abnormal brain activity which eliminated alcohol as a cause. As I have mentioned, I finally had a beer some 3 months after my seizure. As always I gradually began drinking more and quickly got to the point where I was drinking vodka again. On one occasion Katie had me talk to a social worker at one of the hospitals. The social worker explained that I had to get off alcohol before they could treat me for anything. She mentioned that the hospital had a six day detox program and that after insurance paid, my portion of the debt would be $125 per day. I told her that before I went into their detox center that I needed to see if I could detox myself. Just before Christmas of 2003 I did my six days of not drinking. This showed that I didn't need the 6 day program. I had a hard time but did manage to make it through the 6 days. However after the 6 days I soon picked up my drinking right where I had left it.

I had been diagnosed with bipolar disorder but saw very little of the manic phase. I was, however, extremely depressed and seemed to get at least a temporary respite via alcohol. In the meantime my psychiatrist was trying all kinds of ant-depressant medications on me but nothing seemed to work. In retrospect I wonder how many of these medications were being affected by my alcohol intake. Anyway I'm thinking that my next step, if needed will be electro-shock therapy, Then again, perhaps the fact that I haven't been drinking may help me sort things out so that the electro-shock may not be needed. As the year 2004 arrived I began to drink heavily. This time my boys' began getting into the arguments along with my wife. Of course they wanted me to stop drinking. My oldest son mentioned that he had wanted to have a barbeque at our place but he was afraid of the condition that I might be in. I knew I had to start a supreme effort to quit drinking but couldn't get out of the rut I was in. I was now buying half-gallons of vodka so that I wouldn't have to go the liquor store so often. I remember going to the liquor store one Tuesday when I was completely out of vodka. The liquor store was closed for elections and I almost began crying. I thought that I was passed the point where I could just drink beer to get by. My drinking had advanced to the point that I knew I needed to quit. once and for all. I was now to the point where I was drinking at least a fifth per day, My mornings no longer started with a cup of coffee but I would immediately get my bottle. I'd have one drink and then throw it up—then a second which I would also throw up Then I would wait a couple of minutes and the third drink would stay down. For the rest of the day I wouldn't get tanked but I would certainly maintain the level of alcohol in my bloodstream. I would try and time my naps so that I would still be sleeping when Katie came home from work. After arising I would greet Katie and then have a wake-up drink as soon as I could. By this time I had bottles stashed all over the house in places where Katie was unlikely to look. There is another trait of an alcoholic—stashing bottles and alcoholics become ingenious at doing this. I've already mentioned that I had a bottle stashed in the toilet tank. Needless to say I would never been able to get through a job interview at this time but I was still sending out my resume.

Toward the end of June I decided that I had to quite drinking and quit forever as one drink or a single beer would set me off all over again. I named July 2 as my start and restricted my drinking to beer until then. On July 1 tried to drink a 12 pack of beer but couldn't keep it down. I would have a beer then immediately throw it up. I went through the whole 12 pack in this fashion. The next day was my starting day for not drinking and wasn't sure that I was ready. Finally I told myself that I would have to go through the detox stage sooner or later and that I might as well get it over with. The next week was pure hell and I almost had Katie take me to the 6 day detox center that I mentioned earlier. In the second week I felt somewhat better but still had an enormous craving for alcohol. I decided to try the 12 steps of AA.

The first step states that we must admit that we are powerless over alcohol and that our lives had become unmanageable. This was a step that held me back for many years. I had always felt that I had some measure of control as I could cut down when I wanted to, etc. However, during my last bout with drinking I learned that I am indeed powerless over alcohol. If I had a bottle I would start drinking as soon as I got up in the morning. If I didn't have a bottle I would be frantically pacing the floor until 10.00 A.M. when the liquor store opened. I could affect my drinking for a short time but not over any appreciable time. I would always eventually fail. As I have said I was a "functional" alcoholic in that I could at least hold onto a job and perform well, However one needs to look at would happen on weekends and holidays. Also look what has happened to me since I've been out of a job. I've felt that I had nothing to do but drink. In conclusion I can only admit that, at least in the long run, I am indeed powerless over alcohol.

The second step is to believe that a power greater than ourselves can restore us to sanity. My higher power is God and I believe that

He can certainly restore us to sanity. My question is what will prompt him to do this. I guess that's where the other steps come in.

Step 3 is make a decision to turn over our will and our lives over to the care if God as we understood him. I did indeed make this decision but did not entirely turn my life over to God. What I did turn over through prayer was my alcoholism. I had a terrible craving for alcohol that night but it was gone the next morning and has not returned. I am well aware of the fact that I may still weaken at times but I'm trusting God to help me through such times.

I'm certainly no expert when it comes to the 12 steps. All I can do is be sincere in trying to follow through with them. I will by no means become complacent with my alcoholism.

There was a counselor at St. Benedicts who made a very interesting comment. She said that she was glad that she was an alcoholic—that she would never have become the person she is now without alcohol. As far as myself I'm going to try to keep away from alcohol as long as I live and trust in God for the rest. As I see it right now I have only two things for which I can thank alcohol. The first is the fact that I would never have met my wife if I hadn't been in a slightly intoxicated state. The second thing is that after seeing me go through what I have been through my sons will most likely never become alcoholics.

2

TRICKS OF THE ALCOHOLIC MIND

Alcohol is a cruel master—even more so because it let's you think you are master. You are the one that's in control and you can take booze or leave it. Alcohol also has no pride and is perfectly willing to allow you to make such statements—even if you're lying in the gutter in your own vomit. Even in that state alcohol is not your master. All you need is a little time to get back on your feet. I lived under the myth that I could control alcohol for some 20 years. All that time I felt like I could quit anytime I really meant to. Alcohol wants you to have these kinds of thoughts and to feel superior to it. If we sometimes slip and overdo it a little that's no big deal. We'll just be a little more careful next time. Even if you reach the point where you fear that alcohol is taking you over—don't despair. As soon as you can marshal together all of your forces together you can lick alcohol once and for all. You may even be able to have an occasional drink and still maintain control. I'm going to start getting ready for the big effort tomorrow. I might as well have a few more tonight because the time is drawing nigh and I probably won't even want to drink shortly. Alcohol works this way—it's always tomorrow. In fact it can be worse than this. I remember one time when I became totally disgusted with myself and poured a fifth of vodka down the drain—more or less in the throes of some kind of attack of righteous indignation. I felt great about having the pure guts to do something like that and really mean it. This feeling lasted for all of 5 minutes before the doubts started to creep in. Perhaps I hadn't been quite ready to take such drastic action. Probably it'll be a lot easier when I'm under less pressure. Why can't we see that such a time will never come? There will always be some kind of pressure or something that will give you the idea that things will be a lot easier if you just wait for such and such to happen.

Alcohol has quite an arsenal of weapons but procrastination is probably the bazooka of the bunch. I find myself even procrastinating procrastination. Before the original time even arrives I'm already equipped with enough excuses to warrant another delay—of course this will be the last one. regardless. When I was younger I would do the following at least once a week. I'd buy a new notebook and write a page about what I planned to accomplish during the period that the notebook would cover. I'd number out 100 pages or so (depending upon how big the notebook was) and leave some room at the end for an evaluation for the period. Once I got through a whole week before I tore out my "title page", wrote a new one, and renumbered my pages. When things got too messy I would just buy a new notebook. I had other goals aside from not drinking but it was always just before or after a big drunk that I would rip out my now outdated title sheet. I still think the idea is a good one but you must be brutally honest with yourself. If you do well congratulate yourself (but not with a cognac) I've heard people say that you should pat yourself on the back after getting through a tough day. I say never pat yourself on the back. Alcohol may have put a knife in your hand.

I hate to use other people's slogans, etc, and not only because of the legal dangers but because I like to think of myself as original. Anyway I have a thought about getting out of this procrastination loop. Get yourself a big pot and pour in it all of your worries, anxieties, fears, prejudices, etc. Next start a big flame under the pot and JUST STEW IT. Slur your words a little and don't expect me to believe you've never slurred before.

Let me pursue the notebook idea a little further as it's something I plan to do—I have to procrastinate a little because it's 2;00 A.M. and 7-11 doesn't have the kind of notebook I'm looking for. I want something that is bound and looks official—something you would never even consider tearing a page from. On the first page I will write down whatever I plan to accomplish during the period covered by the book. Not drinking will be my first notation. And I may put down some more things…. The whole idea here is not ever to start over again. Even if I slip regarding my drinking I won't start again. I'll write about the slip—everything about it. Perhaps it will help in the future. I will keep track of my feelings about drinking. One caveat:;. I don't care if I use the book for other things that I want to keep trying. I just don't want myself mutilating or throwing the book away because I gained 10 lbs. or something like that. This is primarily my DRINKING JOUNAL and perhaps that's all it should be.

The alcoholic mind is a true marvel. If its skill at self-preservation and just plain ingenuity could somehow be channeled we would be living in an entirely different world. It is almost unbelievable how alcoholism can take over every facet of one's life. As for myself I can only say that almost every decision that I make is somehow based on or at least is involved with my drinking. Anytime we plan to go somewhere my first thought is "Will I be able to drink?" or "How long will I have to go without drinking? I don't really care much about having money in my wallet as long as I have enough to buy a pint. Recently I've begun to write checks or use a credit card at liquor stores. This is something I always told myself I would never do. If we happen to be going to a party or something like that my first question Is always "Will there be booze there? I've always possessed a certain amount of pride but even that is rapidly disappearing as I realize that I would actually beg for alcohol. I'm just one step above the winos that hang around liquor stores asking for spare change.

Alcohol makes liars of us all. When asked "how much did you have to drink?" my standard reply is "just a few beers". This answer brings up the issue of golf because I unfailingly give this answer to what I consider to be a minor version of the Spanish Inquisition. One time I remember tripping over my clubs as I was trying to carry them into the house. Still it was a matter of "just a few beers with the guys". I've always noticed that you're a little better off if you don't admit that you were drinking alone. Golf can be a problem if you need something stronger than beer. I used to buy a couple of beers before starting. I would drink one and put the other in my bag. If we happened to be playing 18 holes I would do the same between the two rounds. After the round everyone would sit around and drink beer anyway. For the last several years I have always needed something stronger. Therefore I'd have a bottle in the car when I arrived at the golf course. I'd have a good straight hit before I even got my clubs out of the car. I would still follow along with the beer thing but it wasn't such a big deal anymore. After the round I would have another good snort as I was putting my clubs in the car.

Then I would return to the clubhouse and have a beer with the guys—a beer that I could even nurse if I didn't care to get into the round-buying routine. On the way home I would drink some more and then lie to my wife about "just having a few with the boys"

At one time I thought I had the complete answer for drinking and golf. I got a new bag that had a built-in compartment for a water bottle. Then all I had to do was fill the bottle with straight vodka. Then I was playing with my youngest son one day and he asked if he could have a drink out of my bottle. Fortunately there just happened to be a concession truck approaching us so I just said "Let's get you something cold." thus escaping my predicament. Since then I've been a little leery of carrying vodka in my water bottle. Even I am unable to keep from gasping after a drink of warm vodka.

The alcoholic mind really show its mettle when it comes to stashing bottles. The biggest problem is remembering where they're stashed and this can sometimes be a very crucial situation. The problem is that your alcoholic mind is far superior to your normal mind and for some reason your alcoholic mind will not help in finding stashed bottles. Apparently it feels that it has already done enough for you in stashing the bottle in the first place.

Occasionally even the alcoholic mind can be overcome by the irrational and capricious mind of a woman. Why on earth should she insist on cleaning off a certain shelf even though it hasn't been cleaned in years.? Why should she happen to look in one of your shoeboxes in the closet? The list goes on and on and it is a never-ending battle. Once I thought I was entirely safe when I put a bottle in my car trunk underneath the spare tire which also had a cover

over it. Then what happens—I'm with my wife when I get a flat tire and my wife insists on helping me change it.

I've given up on the "Oh, that's probably been there for years" which I used to used in the old days. Your wife will simply say "Then how come it wasn't there yesterday" Back in the old days I actually had a liquor cabinet. Even then I would play games. When I had too much vodka I would simply pour some water in the bottle. This did get a little embarrassing one time when a friend of Katie's asked for a bloody mary, Fortunately they then left the room as I had to half fill the glass with my watery vodka. The fact that I had some colored glasses also helped tremendously.

I also used to use alcohol as a reward. This has been something very difficult for me to overcome. It used to that "once I get these bills paid I'm going to make myself a good strong drink', of after I get the grass cut, etc. Without booze to look forward to I find that it's much harder to get started on anything. A glass of iced tea just doesn't do it for me. In looking back I more or less worked on some kind of perverted reward scheme. Otherwise I would never have accomplished anything at all. As it was I could do almost anything as long as there was a drink waiting at the end.

3

HEALTH CONCERNS

At one time alcoholism was thought of as a symptom of stress or as a learned, coping behavior. More recently it has come to be viewed as a complex disease in its own right. Alcohol has direct toxic as well as sedative effects on the body. Failure to take care of nutritional and physical needs during long periods of excessive drinking further complicate matters. Advanced cases often require hospitalization. Effects on major organ systems are cumulative and include a wide range of digestive system disorders such as ulcers, inflammation of the pancreas and cirrhosis of the liver. The control and peripheral nervous systems can be permanently damaged. Blackouts, hallucinations and extreme terror can occur. The latter symptoms are involved in the most serious alcohol withdrawal syndrome, delirium tremens which can prove fatal if not treated or treated incorrectly.

Consumed in moderate amounts alcoholic beverages are relaxing and in some cases may even have beneficial effects on health.

Alcohol is a factor in more than half of the countries homicides, suicides and traffic accidents. Nearly 100,000 Americans die per year as a result of alcohol abuse. Many law enforcement agencies regard a .08 % of alcohol in the bloodstream as evidence of intoxication. Some physical ailments that alcohol can lead to are hypoglycemia, brain and heart damage, enlarged blood vessels in the skin, and chronic gastritus of the pancreas…Alcoholism may lead to impotence in man, and damage to the fetus in women There is also an elevated risk of cancer of the larynx, esophagus, stomach, pancreas and upper gastrointestinal tract. Since alcoholics seldom have adequate diets they are likely to have nutritional deficiencies. Heavy drinkers have impaired liver function and least one in five develop cirrhosis…

The cause of alcoholism seems to a blend of genetic, physical, psychological, environment and social factors that vary among individuals. Genetic factors are considered crucial. A given person's risk of becoming an alcoholic is four to five times greater if a parent is an alcoholic. Some children of alcoholics, however overcome the hereditary pattern by becoming teetotalers…At one time alcoholism was thought of a matter of weakness—something that could be overcome with will power. More recently it has been classified as a complex disease that has nothing o do with will power. To summarize what I have stated above and as far as health, alcohol can cause the following:

1. impotence in men

2. damage to a fetus in women.

3. hypoglycemia

4. enlarged blood vessels in the skin

5. pancreatitus

6. ulcers

7. cirrhosis of the liver (1 out of 5 alcoholics develop this)

8. elevated risk of cancer of the larynx, esophagus, pancreas and upper gastrointestinal tract

9. permanent damage to the central and peripheral nervous systems

10. brain damage

11. damage to immune system

Studies have shown that moderate drinker—men who have two or less drinks per day (one for women) are less likely to die from one form of heart disease. It is believed that these smaller amounts of alcohol protect help protect against heart disease by changing the blood's chemistry, thus reducing the risk of blood clots in the heart. This does not mean that non-drinkers should start drinking.

A drink is considered to be one 12 ounce can of beer.

Following is a list of facts about alcohol:

1. Alcoholism does run in families and researches are working to discover the actual genes that are involved

2. heavy drinking can increase the risk for certain cancers, especially those of the liver, esophagus, throat and larynx (voice box)—heavy drinking can also cause liver cirrhosis, immune system problems, brain damage and harm to the fetus during pregnancy

3. both homicide and suicide are more likely to be committed by people who have been drinking automobile crashes and on-the-job injuries

4. 1 out of 13 Americans abuse alcohol (14 million Americans)

5. in purely economic terms alcohol costs society 185 billion dollars per year

6. alcoholism has nothing to do with will power

7. the need can be as great as the need for food and water

8. alcoholics are in the grip of an uncontrollable need

9. there is a difference between alcohol abuse and alcoholism in that abuse doesn't involve the uncontrollable need or craving

10. however the effects of alcohol abuse are also experienced by alcoholics

11. Treatment may include detoxification (the process of safely getting alcohol out of your system); taking doctor-prescribed medications, such as disulfiram (Antabuse®) or naltrexone (ReVia™), to help prevent a return (or relapse) to drinking once drinking has stopped

12. Studies have shown that moderate drinkers—men who have two or less drinks per day and women who have one or less drinks per day are less likely to die from one form of heart disease than are people who do not drink any alcohol or who drink more. It's believed that these smaller amounts of alcohol help protect against heart disease by changing the blood's chemistry, thus reducing the risk of blood clots in the heart's arteries. This is not to say that if you are a non-drinker that you should start.

13. More than 250 medications interact harmfully with alcohol. These interactions may result in increased risk of illness, injury, and even death. Alcohol's effects are heightened by medicines that depress the central nervous system, such as sleeping pills, antihistamines, antidepressants, anti-anxiety drugs, and some painkillers. In addition, medicines for cer-

tain disorders, including diabetes, high blood pressure, and heart disease, can have harmful interactions with alcohol. If you are taking any

14. risk is not destiny

15. An estimated 17.6 million American adults meet standard diagnostic criteria for an alcohol use disorder and approximately 4.2 million meet criteria for a drug use disorder. Marketed as ReVia by Dupont-Merck, naltrexone has a former life as Trexan, also marketed by Dupont. It is the first medication, since the development of disulfiram in the 1950s, to be approved specifically for the treatment of alcoholism

16. The 1990s brought revolutionary change to alcoholism treatment. As the decade began, one medication; disulfiram (Antabuse) was approved for the treatment of alcoholism.

17. Approximately 10% of people who regularly drink alcohol will develop alcohol dependence

18. Alcohol treatment includes the use of thiamine and foliate to prevent the development of Wernicke-Korsakoff syndrome

19. Five percent of Americans die of alcoholism.

All of the above statistics mean nothing when applied to an individual. I think the true alcoholic doesn't care whether he lives or dies. However I think most of us want to live. Let's get about that business shall we?

How about some more nasty statistics:

…

According to the National Council on Alcoholism and Drug Dependence, about 18 million Americans abuse alcohol. Each year more than 100,000 Americans die of alcohol-related causes. Alcohol is a factor in nearly half of all traffic deaths.

Some additional facts (some of which are redundant but cannot be overstressed):

1. There is a difference between alcoholics and alcohol abusers in that abusers don't have the uncontrollable craving for alcohol that alcoholics do. However alcoholics can also be alcohol abusers.

2. The need for alcohol can be as great as the need for food and water

3. alcoholism does run in families and researchers are working to discover the actual genes involved

4. 1 of 13 Americans abuse alcohol (14 million Americans)

5. in purely economic terms alcohol costs society 185 billion dollars per year

6. alcoholism has nothing to do with will power

7. alcoholics are in the grip of an uncontrollable need

8. 100,000 die per year as a result of alcohol abuse

9. Many law enforcement agencies regard a,08 % of alcohol in the bloodstream as evidence of intoxication

10. the risk of a person becoming an alcoholic is 4 to 5 times greater if a parent is an alcoholic—some children avoid this hereditary pattern by becoming teetotalers

11. more than 250 medications interact harmfully with alcohol

12. 18 million Americans have alcohol problems

13. five percent of Americans die of alcoholism

14. approximately 10% of people who regularly drink become alcoholics

15. Alcohol is a factor in nearly half of all traffic deaths

16. delirium tremens can prove fatal if not treated or treated incorrectly

17. alcohol is involved with 50% of suicides and homicides

18. Two drugs have been approved for alcohol abuse in the U.S. The first disulfiram (Antabuse) was approved in the 1950s. Another drug, naltrexone in the 90's.

19. Since alcoholics seldom have adequate diets they are likely to have nutritional deficiencies.

4

ALCOHOL ANONYMOUS AND THE TWELVE STEPS

The story of AA begins in 1935 at a meeting between Bill W., a New York stockbroker and Bob W., an Akron physician. Their meeting took place in Akron, Ohio. Six months earlier the stock broker was relieved of his drink obsession by a sudden spiritual experience following a meeting with an alcoholic friend who had been in touch with the Oxford groups of that time. The stock broker had also been greatly helped. By Dr. William D. Silkworth a specialist in alcoholism who is now considered a medical saint. From this doctor the broker had learned of the grave nature of alcoholism. The stock broker could not accept all of the tenets of the Oxford groups but he was convinced of the need for moral inventory, confessing of personality defects, restitution to those harmed, helpfulness to others and the necessity of belief in and dependence upon God.

Prior to his trip to Akron, the stock broker had worked hard with many alcoholics, on the theory that only an alcoholic could help another alcoholic. His only success was in keeping himself sober.

A failed business made the broker afraid that he might start drinking again. He suddenly realized that in order to save himself he must carry the message to another alcoholic. That alcoholic turned out to be the Akron physician who had repeatedly tried spiritual means to resolve his alcoholic dilemma but had failed. But when the broker gave him Dr. Silkworth's description of alcoholism and its hopelessness, the physician began to pursue the spiritual remedy for his malady with a willingness that he had never been able to muster. He recovered. He never had another drink up to his death in 1950. This seemed to prove that one alcoholic could affect another as no nonalcoholic could. It also indicated that strenuous work, one alcoholic with another, was vital to permanent recovery. The two men set to work almost frantically upon alcoholics arriving in the ward of the Akron City Hospital. Their very first case, a desperate one, recovered almost immediately and became AA member number 3.

This work at Akron continued through the summer of 1935. When the stock broker returned to New York in the fall the first AA group had formed although no one realized it at the time.

By late 1937, the number of members having substantial sobriety time behind them was sufficient to convince the member that a new light had entered the dark world of the alcoholic. Other groups began springing up and the struggling groups thought that it was time to place their message before the world. Thus the "big book" was born. The membership had then reached about 100 men and women. The fledgling society, nameless at this time, adopted the name "Alcoholics Anonymous" from the title of its own book. The book was published in 1939. By March 1941 the membership had soared to 2000. By the end of 1941 an estimate 8000 were on their way to recovery. By March when the 3rd edition of the big book was published membership was conservatively estimated at a million with about 20,000 in 91 countries. By 1980 there were 40,000 groups in 106 countries. There are now 2 million members.

As the society grew it was time to face the problems of organization. This was the. the substance of AA's

Twelve Traditions (not to be confused with the 12 steps to recovery.). The goal was to evolve principles by which the AA groups and AA as a whole could survive and function effectively. These are:

1. Our common welfare should come first, personal recovery depends upon AA unity.

2. For our group purpose there is but one ultimate authority—a loving God as He may express Himself in our group conscience. Our leaders are but trusted servants; they do not govern

3. The only requirement for AA membership is a desire to stop drinking

4. Each group should be autonomous except in matters affecting other groups or AA as a whole.

5. Each group has but one primary purpose—to carry its message to the alcoholic who still suffers.

6. A group ought never endorse, finance or lend the AA name to any related facility or outside enterprise, lest problems of money, property and prestige divert us from our primary purpose.

7. Every AA group ought to be fully self-supporting, declining outside contributions.

8. Alcohols Anonymous should forever nonprofessional, but our service may employ special workers,

9. AA, as such, ought never be organized; but we may create service boards or committees directly responsible to those they serve.

10. Alcoholics Anonymous has no opinion on outside issues; hence the AA name ought never be drawn into public controversy.

11. Our public relations policy is based on attraction rather then promotion; we need always maintain personal anonymity at the level of press, radio and films.

12. Anonymity is the spiritual foundation of all our traditions reminding us to place principles before personalities.

The above is the short version of the Twelve Traditions. For the long version see page 565 of the big book. As mentioned the first edition of the big book," Alcoholics Anonymous" was published in 1939. The second edition was published in 1955 and 1,150,000 were sold. The third edition was published in 1976. Only minor changes were made for each edition...For example some of the stories were changed. The section called "The Doctors Opinion" has remained intact from the first edition. This was written in 1939 by the late Dr. William D, Silkworth who was the society's great benefactor. The second edition added the appendices, the Twelve Traditions and directions for getting in touch with AA. Still the biggest change was in the section personal stories which was expanded to reflect the fellowship's growth. Seven stories were retained from the first edition. Thirty new stories were added and the story section was divided into 3 sections. For the third edition 8 new stories were added. All changes over the years have been aimed at representing the current member ship of AA and thereby to reach more alcoholics. The "big book" serves as a sort of bible for AA.

A board of trustees administers the organization and activities in the U.S and Canada. The board consists of 7 nonalcoholics and 14 AA members. Regional delegates vote on matters of general significance at annual conferences. An international conference is held every 5 years.

AA maintains an archive which is the repository of personal collections, manuscripts, publifatios, photographs and memorabilia related to the origin and development of AA. The archivist's job is to receive. classify and indeed all relevant material such as administrative files and records, correspondence, and artifactual works considered to have historical input to AA. Access to AA members is provided as determined by the archivist in consultation with the trustee Archive committee.

Now I'm going to discuss the 12 steps to recovery. Three main ideas can be distilled from the 12 steps:

1. That we were alcoholic and could not manage our own lives.

2. That probably no human could have relieved our alcoholism.

3. That God could and would if He were sought.

Now I'd like to go through the steps individually and note what progress I have made:

Step #1

We admitted we were powerless over alcohol—that our lives had become unmanageable.

Result:

This was a very difficult step for me—due largely to the fact that I was a functional alcoholic for so many years. I'd drink one day, cut down one day and go a day without. Often though. I have to think of the last days before I quit. When I awoke in the morning I would do one of two things: If I had a bottle I would immediately start drinking. I wouldn't even bother to have a cup of coffee. I would drink until about 9:00 A.M. then go back to bed for a while. If I didn't have a bottle I would more or less pace the floor until 10 A, M. and the liquor stores opened. For some time I wouldn't go until 10:15 A.M. as I didn't want to appear too anxious. However as time went on I gave up this little ruse and was often to be found sitting in the parking lot just waiting for the store to open. Towards the last days I would always buy a half-gallon which would only last for two days, This meant that I was drinking about a quart a day, I always had a partially empty 12 pack of beer at the bottom of the stairs in the garage. That way if I Katie asked me if I had been drinking I could say yes but only beer. Alcohol makes you a sneak and a liar. I never lied to my wife except when it came to drinking. Then I would lie and sometimes get caught in my own lies. I had bottle scattered all over the house in places where I didn't think she'd look. I even had one in the toilet tank at one time. Sometimes Katie would find one of my stashed bottles. I would then say that I couldn't remember when I had stashed it. I would eventually end up in a trap with all my lies and then I would say that I was sick of drinking and was going to do something about it. Katie would ask when I would give her a date in the nearby future. Then when the date came I would think or a reason to push the date forward. I would often use work as an alibi, saying that I was under unusually high pressure and would be in a position to quit after the pressure was off.

Every once in a while I would go somewhere with Katie and not drink at all in an appeasement gesture. She would always be pleasantly surprised and I would be able to drink for few days afterward. Alcohol make you into a cheat and a liar. Even if you don't lie about anything else.

I might add that I wasn't getting all that drunk even though towards the end I was drinking a quart per day. Katie and the kids would still notice—all Katie had to do was to look at me. One thing I really disliked was the fact that she would often kiss me when arriving home from work—not that she wanted to kiss me—she just wanted to taste my breath in order to tell if I had been drinking or not.

Step #2

Came to believe that a power greater then ourselves could restore us to sanity.

Result:

This was no problem for me as I have always believed in God and the simple that he can do anything he wants. My only question was why he should choose to help me. Here the religious conflicts in my head came to the fore. If I was a sinner in the eyes of God for not being a good Mormon then how could I expect Him to help me. Of course drinking is a sin in the Mormon church so perhaps God would help me on this basis. I must admit, however, that I was not attempting to quit because drinking was considered a sin in the

Morman church. I was instead trying to quit for my own self and my family.

Step #3

Made a decision to turn our will and our lives over to the care of God as we understood him.

Result:

I did turn my drinking problem over to God—in fact I made a promise the I would do all in my power not to drink. In return I asked God to help me over the rough spots. I realize that you can't bargain with God but this seemed right for me. Despite my one-sided pact I could not absolutely depend upon God to do what I more or less demanded. However I do believe in a loving God and One that will help us in righteous causes. If drinking was not a sin it then, at least it lead to sin—lying, cheating. etc., Also what would have happened if, while intoxicated, I happened to cause a car wreck and someone was killed. I would never get over something like that. I actually get shivers just thinking about all the luck that made this not happen, Even if I fail in my quest to drinking I hereby state that I will never again drive a vehicle when intoxicated.

Step #4

Made a searching and fearless moral inventory of ourselves.

Result:

I am still working on this. The first thing I note is that I'm self-ish—not about material things but in particular my time. Often I felt that my drinking time was being infringed upon. This goes along with my second shortcoming—I'm not a very sociable person. This can be good and bad—bad because Katie is very sociable and I hold her back in many ways. Most of my other shortcomings are a direct result of my alcoholism.

Step #5

Admitted to God, to ourselves and to other human being the exact nature of our wrongs.

Result:

I have admitted to God and myself the nature of my wrongs. I have admitted these things to Katie but only when drinking. I need to do this when sober.

Step #6

Were entirely ready to have God remover all these defects of character.

Result:

Once again I was only willing to have God remove the burden of alcohol. In doing this I feel that most of my shortcomings have to do with alcohol.

Step #7

Humbly asked Him to remove our shortcomings.

Result:

I prayed almost constantly that the burden of alcohol be removed from me but did not mention my other shortcomings. Perhaps I simply wasn't sincere enough. I think I was more or less asking God to let me drink moderately. One night I must have gotten it right. I went to bed with a bad craving for alcohol. The next morning the craving was gone.

Step #8

Made a list of all persons we had harmed, and became willing to make amends to them all. The primary people I have harmed are my family. I am certainly willing to make amends to them. I must consider my parents even though they are with Thee. I still want them to be proud of me. My brother and sisters have also been embarrassed by my behavior. The only thing I can do as far as making amends is to not do it again.

Step #9

Made direct amends to such people wherever possible, except when to do so would injure them or others.

Result:

For the most part making direct amends is a matter of not doing these things again. I will apologize to these people as the opportunities to do so come along. I'm not ready to call the whole family together although this may be what I should do.

Step #10

Continued to take personal inventory and when we were wrong promptly admitted it.

Result:

I am currently attempting to do this.

Step #11

Sought through prayer and meditation to improve our conscious contact with God as we understood Him, praying only for knowledge of His will for us and the power to carry that out.

Result:

I am currently trying to do this.

Step #12

Having had a spiritual awakening as the result of these steps, we tried to carry this message to alcoholics, and to practice these principles in all our affairs.

Result:

Once again I'm trying to do this. As far as carrying the message I think I need to go to an AA meeting and not only listen but speak.

5

A BRIEF HISTORY OF ALCOHOL

No one knows when alcoholic beverages were first discovered. Probably some people living in a hot climate ate some grapes or berries that had begun to rot and liked the taste. Tiny yeast spores change sugar in fruits, berries or honey into alcohol and carbon dioxide through a process called fermentation. Over 5,000 years ago people were making alcoholic beverages. Before they used grapes to make wine they used starchy gains like wheat and barley. Beer became the drink of the common people in many parts if the world. Clean drinking water was hard to find so people drank beer. Beer was actually a food at that time. Most modern beers are thin but not the beer that was made then. We don't know how people learned to make distilled alcohols as it required great skill. First a liquid such as beer or wine was boiled. Then the cooled vapors and condensed and concentrated and impurities removed.

Early settlers in North America began making alcoholic beverages from apples, grapes, berries, carrot, celery, or spinach and also used grains. By the early 1700s settlers had learned to distill rye and barley into whisky. By 1780 whiskey and bourbon were being made from corn. Early Americans liked to drink and Thomas Jefferson claimed that one-third of the U.S. was killing itself with whiskey. In

1830 Americans were drinking three times more per capita than they are now.

During the 1800s the temperance movement began to grow. Mostly members of the movement wanted moderation rather then abstinence. In 1919 both the House and the Senate passed to 18th Amendment to the constitution which said that no alcohol could be manufactured. imported, exported, transported or sold in the United States. The movement was a failure and was repealed in 1933 with the 21rst Amendment.

Ethyl alcohol or ethanol is a thin, colorless liquid with little or no odor. It has no vitamins, minerals, or nutrients. All alcohol is made the same way—from fermentation or the process of yeast changing sugars into ethyl alcohol. The body removes alcohol in two ways: excretion and metabolism. Only 10% of alcohol is excreted through urine, breath, saliva, or sweat. The other 90% remains in the body until enzymes or complex proteins in the liver break down the alcohol into water and carbon dioxide. The liver is the only organ that breaks down alcohol. The liver can break down the half an ounce of alcohol in a 12 ounce beer in about an hour and half.

Each year the average American adult drinks 2.75 gallons of distilled spirits, 2.77 gallons of wine, and 30.4 gallons of beer.

6

<u>SOME SUGGESTIONS</u>

I have found that the following help me with alcohol cravings. This certainly does not mean that they will help anyone else but I am offering them anyway.

In general I think that anything that keeps you busy is good—anything that keeps you mind active. In particular I have found that all of the following have helped me.

1. AA meetings

2. Call an alcoholic friend

3. Try to help another alcoholic

4. Get a hobby

5. Start a project such as building a deck

6. Listen to soothing music

7. Get a dog

8. Relaxation therapy or yoga

9. Jogging

10. Working with weights

11. Reading

The above are just suggestions and you can certainly substitute at will. I didn't mention sewing as that would probably drive me to drink. I've got to stop writing now or I'll go on forever. Please be aware that I'm not trying to be facetious. However I am well aware of the fact that you should never take yourself too seriously.

BIBLIOGRAPHY

Alcoholics Anonymous(3rd ed.), New York, Alcoholics Anonymous World Services, 1976

Twelve Steps and Twelve Traditions (3rd ed.) New York Alcoholics Anonymous World Services, 1981

Judge, Mark Gauvreau, Wasted, Hazeldon, Center Center, Minnesota, 1997

Knapp, Caroline, Drinking A Love Story, New York, The Dial Press, 1996

Maxwell, Milton A., The AA Experience, The Book Press,1976

Graham, James, The Secret History of Alcoholism, Rockport, MA, Element Books Limited, 1996

Ragge, Ken, The Real AA, Tucson, Arizona, Sharp Press,1998

"Alcoholism", Func & Wagnalls New Encyclopedia, New York

Peacock, Nancy, Drowning Our Sorrows, Philadelphia, Chelsea House Publishers, 2000

0-595-33177-7